free

D0246138

WEALTH, POVERTY & WELFARE

Tony Cole

Series Editor: Paul Selfe

Hodder & Stoughton

A MEMBER OF THE HODDER HEADLINE GROUP

ACKNOWLEDGEMENTS

The publishers would like to thank the following for granting permission to use photos:

"PA" Photos: page 12
Life File: pages 50 and 82
The Department for Education and Employment: page 131.

The author would like to thank Epping Forest College.

DEDICATION

For Gerison, Francine and Georgia – and my parents.

Orders: please contact Bookpoint Ltd, 39 Milton Park, Abingdon, Oxon OX14 4TD. Telephone: (44) 01235 400414, Fax: (44) 01235 400454. Lines are open from 9.00–6.00, Monday to Saturday, with a 24 hour message answering service. Email address: orders@bookpoint.co.uk

A catalogue record for this title is available from The British Library

ISBN 0 340 72056 5

First published 1999
Impression number 10 9 8 7 6 5 4 3 2 1
Year   2005 2004 2003 2002 2001 2000 1999

Cover photo from Life File

Typeset by Transet Limited, Coventry, England.
Printed in Great Britain for Hodder & Stoughton Educational, a division of Hodder Headline plc, 338 Euston Road, London NW1 3BH by Redwood Books, Trowbridge, Wilts.

CONTENTS

1

INTRODUCTION

HOW TO USE THE BOOK

EACH CHAPTER IN this book examines one or more of the central debates relating to the sociology of inequality and welfare. The text is devised for readers with little or no background knowledge in the subject, and there are Study Points and Activities throughout to encourage a consideration of the issues raised. Student readers are advised to make use of these and answer them either on paper or in group discussion, a particularly fruitful way of learning; they will assist them to develop the skills of interpretation, analysis and evaluation. There are many ways of preparing for an exam, but a thorough understanding of the material is obviously crucial.

Each chapter is structured to give a clear understanding of the authors, concepts and issues that you need to know about. To assist understanding and facilitate later revision, it is often helpful to make concise notes.

MAKING NOTES FROM THE BOOK

Linear notes
- Bold headings establish key points: names, theories and concepts.
- Subheadings indicate details of relevant issues.
- A few numbered points list related arguments.

Diagram or pattern notes
- Use a large blank sheet of paper and write a key idea in the centre.
- Make links between this and related issues.
- Show also the connections between sub issues which share features in common.

Both systems have their advantages and disadvantages, and may take some time to perfect. Linear notes can be little more than a copy of what is already in the book and patterned notes can be confusing. But if you practise the skills, they can reduce material efficiently and concisely, becoming invaluable for revision. Diagrammatic notes may be very useful for those with a strong visual memory and provide a clear overview of a whole issue, showing patterns of interconnection. The introduction of helpful drawings or a touch of humour into the format is often a good way to facilitate the recall of names, research studies and complex concepts.

Activity

- Make a diagram to show the two ways of making notes with their possible advantages and disadvantages.

SKILLS ADVICE

Students must develop and display certain skills for their examination and recognise which ones are being tested in a question. The clues are frequently in key words in the opening part. The skill domains are:

1 **Knowledge and understanding:** the ability to discuss the views of the main theorists; their similarities and differences; the strengths and weaknesses of evidence. To gain marks students must display this when asked to *explain, examine, suggest a method,* or *outline reasons.*

2 **Interpretation, application and analysis:** the use of evidence in a logical, relevant way, either to show how it supports arguments or refutes them. Students must show this ability when asked *identify, use items A/B/C, draw conclusions from a table.*

3 **Evaluation:** the skill of assessing evidence in a balanced way so that logical conclusions follow. Students can recognise this skill when asked to *assess, critically examine, comment on levels of reliability, compare and contrast,* or if asked *to what extent.*

Activity

Draw an evaluation table, as below, using the whole of an A4 page. Examine studies as you proceed in your work and fill in the relevant details. Keep it for revision purposes.

Sociologist		
Title of the study	Strengths	Weaknesses
Verdict		
Judgement/justification		

REVISION ADVICE

- Keep clear notes at all times in a file or on disk (with back up copy).
- Be familiar with exam papers and their demands.
- Become familiar with key authors, their theories, their research and sociological concepts.

Activity
Make and keep **Key Concept Cards**, as shown below.

COLLECTIVE CONSCIENCE

Key idea

A term used by **Durkheim** meaning:

- The existence of a social and moral order exterior to individuals and acting upon them as an independent force.
- The shared sentiments, beliefs and values of individuals which make up the **collective conscience.**
- In **traditional societies** it forms the basis of social order.
- As societies modernise the collective conscience weakens: **mechanical solidarity** is replaced by **organic solidarity**.

Key theorist: Emile Durkheim

Syllabus area: Functionalism

EXAMINATION ADVICE

To develop an effective method of writing, answers should be:

- **Sociological:** use the language and research findings of sociologists; do not use anecdotal opinion gathered from people not involved in sociology to support arguments.

- **Adequate in length:** ensure enough is written to obtain the marks available.
- **Interconnected:** with other parts of the syllabus (such as stratification, gender, ethnicity).
- **Logical:** the answer follows from the relevant evidence.
- **Balanced:** arguments and counter arguments are weighed; references are suitable.
- **Accurate:** reliable data is obtained from many sources.

The three skill areas on p 2 should be demonstrated, so that the question is answered effectively.

In displaying knowledge, the student is not necessarily also demonstrating interpretation.

- This must be specified with phrases like 'Therefore, this study leads to the view that…'.
- Sections of answers should hang together, one leading to the next. This shows how the question is being answered by a process of analysis based on the evidence.
- Reach a conclusion based on the evidence used and the interpretations made.

The skill of evaluation is often regarded (not necessarily accurately) as the most problematic. Evaluation means being judge and jury; the strengths and weaknesses of evidence are assessed and an overall judgement about its value is made. To evaluate an argument or theory, consider whether it usefully opens up debate and explains the events studied; does it have major weaknesses?

Activity

Look through some past examination papers and pick out the evaluation questions. Underline the evaluation words and work out which skills are required.

COURSEWORK ADVICE

Coursework provides an opportunity to carry out a study using primary and/or secondary data to investigate an issue of sociological interest; it must address theoretical issues. The suggestions included at the end of each chapter may be adapted or used to generate further ideas. Final decisions must be agreed with a teacher or tutor.

MAKING A PLAN

Before starting a piece of coursework, you should make a plan:

1 Read and make notes from articles describing research projects in journals.
2 Have a clear aim in mind; choose an issue that interests you and is within your ability.
3 Decide more precisely what you want to know; establish a simple hypothesis to test.
4 Select a range of possible research methods; consider both quantitative and qualitative techniques.
5 Decide on a range of possible sources of information.
6 List the people from whom you can seek help, perhaps include a statistician.

WRITING THE PROJECT

1 Seek frequent advice from a teacher or tutor.
2 Check the weighting for different objectives in the marking scheme.
3 Keep clear notes throughout, including new ideas and any problems that arise.
4 Limit its length (maximum 5,000 words).
5 Label and index the study in the following way:
   a **Rationale:** a reason for choosing the subject; preliminary observations on the chosen area
   b **Context:** an outline of the theoretical and empirical context of the study
   c **Methodology:** a statement of the methodology used and reasons for selecting it
   d **Content:** presentation of the evidence and/or argument, including results
   e **Evaluation:** the outcomes are weighed and strengths and weaknesses noted.
   f **Sources:** all the sources of information are listed.
OR
   a **Title**
   b **Contents**
   c **Abstract:** a brief summary of the aims, methods, findings and evaluation.
   d **Rationale**
   e **The Study**
   f **Research Diary**
   g **Bibliography**
   h **Appendix:** to include proposal for the study, single examples of a questionnaire or other data-gathering instrument and transcripts of interviews.
   i **Annex:** to include raw data gathered.

Paul Selfe
Series editor

2

INCOME, EMPLOYMENT AND UNEMPLOYMENT

Introduction

THIS CHAPTER IS about the distribution of income. Income is one of the main ways in which people, or institutions, have 'command over economic resources'; the other main one is wealth (Pond, 1989). Income can be defined as a *stream or flow of resources*, whereas wealth is a question of the *ownership* of assets. In practice, the two are often interconnected: income may generate wealth and vice versa; but neither process need occur.

Study point
1   Give *one* reason why income may not necessarily generate wealth.
2   State *two* forms of wealth that can generate income and *two* which do not.

In looking at income and wealth, this chapter – as do others – will explore both structural and locational issues. The former include patterns and trends in the distribution of income and wealth; the latter consider which social groups are most advantaged by these patterns and trends. Explanations of income inequality are also considered, especially those deriving from employment, or the lack of it. Indeed, a whole subsection of this chapter is devoted to unemployment.

Table 1: *Issues, concepts and authors and sources in this chapter*		
KEY ISSUES	KEY CONCEPTS	KEY AUTHORS AND SOURCES
The measurement of income and wealth, including its distribution/redistribution	Original, gross, disposable, post-tax and final income. Real incomes and money incomes. Direct and indirect taxation. Marketable and non-marketable wealth	*Social Trends*
The distribution of income and wealth; trends, patterns associations (class, gender, ethnicity, age) and explanations	Regressive and progressive taxation. Unemployment. Labour-market concepts and theories (dual labour market)	Low Pay Unit Institute of Fiscal Studies Hutton Policy Studies Institute and Labour Force Surveys
Unemployment; unemployment statistics; the social patterning of unemployment rates	Statistics as social constructs; validity and reliability. Economic inactivity	Slattery; dictionaries of sociology. Labour Force Survey; the 'quality' press

SOURCE: *SOCIAL TRENDS*, 26, 1996.

THE DISTRIBUTION OF INCOME

MEASURING INCOME AND ITS DISTRIBUTION

The publication *Social Trends* provides detailed information on the pattern of income distribution and how this is affected by taxes and benefits, including indirect taxes and what are called benefits in kind (ie services like health or education). This is a difficult, highly complicated statistical exercise. It uses official records and survey data on how people spend their money to work out which groups of the population pay most in taxation and which groups gain most from state spending.

The table on page 8 is a condensed version of one in *Social Trends*, 26, 1996. It uses five different measures of income distribution, or rather of redistribution because four of the measures take account of government taxes and benefits on the pattern of distribution. These measures are:

1 *original income*. This comes mostly, but not exclusively, from the market. The market is the arena in which goods and services, including labour, are bought and sold. It is, therefore, the key to an understanding of wages, salaries, fees for services or work, profits, interest on the loan of money, dividends, rents and so on. Original income also includes those market or employment-based incomes such as the imputed money value of benefits in kind (housing coming with job, etc) and of occupational pensions.

Some sources of original income come from outside the market itself, such as maintenance payments between spouses after divorce, but the overall impact of these on the distribution of income is very small.

This category of income measurement does not tell us about the level of income that people actually receive. It is essentially a hypothetical measure that tells us what people *would* get if there were no systems of taxation or welfare.

2 *gross income*. This is simply original income plus any cash benefits people or households receive from the state in so-called transfer payments. There are many forms that this transfer can take. It may be from the rich to the poor, or even vice versa. It may be from the employed to the unemployed; from the sick to the healthy; from the young/employed to the old/retired, and so on.

3 *disposable income*. The previous measure took account of what the state *pays out* in cash benefits. This measure takes account of what it *takes* in taxation, but it only considers taxes on income (e.g. income tax and National Insurance contributions) and local taxes (e.g. council tax, rates).

4 *post-tax income*. This income takes the calculation one step further and measures what is left after indirect taxation has been taken into account as well. The main indirect taxes are VAT on spending and excise duty on products like tobacco and alcohol. This measure has taken all payments of tax to the government into consideration. It has not, however, looked fully at all the benefits that people receive from the state.

5 *final income*. By taking account of the benefits in kind that people receive from the state, this measure does give a full picture of the whole process of redistribution in the tax/benefit system. Using this measure makes it possible to see which income groups gain and which lose from the government tax and benefit system. The relative value of state services to different income groups is considered in Chapter 6.

Table 2: *The distribution of income*

INCOME MEASURE	QUINTILE GROUPS OF HOUSEHOLDS: AVERAGE INCOME PER HOUSEHOLD IN £ PER YEAR, 1994–95					
	BOTTOM FIFTH	NEXT FIFTH	MIDDLE FIFTH	NEXT FIFTH	TOP FIFTH	AVERAGE FOR ALL HOUSEHOLDS
Original income	2,040	5,600	13,380	22,250	40,330	16,720
Gross income	6,700	10,080	16,540	24,200	41,510	19,800
Disposable income	5,860	8,760	13,610	19,150	31,370	15,750
Post-tax income	4,120	6,700	10,520	15,190	26,570	12,620
Final income	7,720	9,840	13,690	17,970	28,640	15,570

SOURCE: *SOCIAL TRENDS*, 26, 1996.

Although Table 2 is a significantly reduced version of the one in *Social Trends*, it still contains a mass of information. However, it will also be better understood with some notes and questions to guide you through it.

Table points to note

1 *Quintiles are statistical categories, each comprising one fifth of the population.*
2 *Measurement by household.*
   a The table deals with the distribution of income by household. This is important to note because households often contain more than one adult with incomes of their own. This makes the quintile income averages higher than they would be if they were just dealing with individuals.
   b It is also important because analysing the distribution of income in this way may lead to an underestimation of the degree of income inequality in the country. An essential concern of feminists has been the way that money is distributed *within*, rather than *between*, households. Women in households with male partners do not always share equally in the household income (Pahl, 1989).
3 *The use of averages.*
   a Household incomes do not just vary *between* quintiles. *Within* each quintile, there will be some households which are above the average for that quintile, and some below it. This is particularly important to bear in mind when considering the top and bottom quintiles. There will be some households in the bottom quintile with *no* original income because they are completely dependent on state benefits; and there will be some in the top quintile, as we shall see, whose incomes are way above the average for that quintile. Having the information in *deciles* instead (ie in sections of one tenth rather than one fifth) would reduce the problem a little because it would give details on smaller groups of the population. The general issue of income inequality within categories would still apply, however.
   b There are different ways of defining the average, as any student of sociology should know. These are the mean, the median and the mode. The one most commonly used, and that employed here, is the mean.

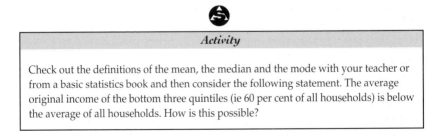

Activity

Check out the definitions of the mean, the median and the mode with your teacher or from a basic statistics book and then consider the following statement. The average original income of the bottom three quintiles (ie 60 per cent of all households) is below the average of all households. How is this possible?

4 *Cross-sectional and time-series data.*

   a Data which gives information about society at one point in time, like the above table, is called *cross-sectional*: it just gives a 'snapshot' of society. It is impossible to tell from the table whether the distribution of income in Britain has become, or is becoming, more egalitarian, or whether the reverse is happening.

   b Data which gives information about society over a certain time period, and preferably at equal and regular intervals, does enable trends to be considered. This is called *time-series data.*

5 *Taxation – progressive and regressive.*

   a Taxes which take a higher proportion of income from higher-income groups are called *progressive taxes*. Those which do the reverse are *regressive*. Income tax, a *direct tax*, has generally been seen as one of the most progressive taxes because there are higher rates for higher earners. For 1999/2000, the top rate of income tax of 40 per cent is levied on taxable incomes above £28,000. This is a marginal rate: all taxable income below that level is taxed at the rates which apply to other earners below that threshold. It should be noted that, by recent historical and current European standards, this is a low threshold for the top rate of tax. It means that the marginal rate of taxation is the same for people on taxable incomes of £280,000 as it is for those on one tenth of that. There was previously a 60 per cent tax rate, but this was abolished in the 1988 Budget, making the tax system much less progressive.

   b Currently, the main regressive taxes are *indirect taxes*, most notably value-added tax (VAT). A simple example will illustrate this. If two people spend £200 each on clothes or household goods, at the current rate of VAT, they both pay £35 in tax. If one of these people receives a weekly income of £200, then that £35 represents 17.5 per cent of their weekly income. If the other person is on £600 per week, that same tax 'bill' represents one third of the proportion of the income of the first person, ie less than 6 per cent. Of course, higher income people pay more VAT *in total* because they spend more, but poorer people tend to pay a higher proportion of their incomes in VAT. The regressive nature of VAT needs to be remembered when looking at one of the most significant tax changes early in Mrs. Thatcher's period of office: the rate of VAT was doubled from 8 per cent to 15 per cent and later increased to 17.5 per cent.

TRENDS IN THE DISTRIBUTION OF INCOME

Trends, watersheds and bias – a brief comment

Trends in the distribution of income may vary according to which income measure is being used. Generally, trends are calculated according to pre-tax and post-tax income, but often only direct taxation is taken into account.

Study point

1 Between which two adjacent quintiles is the income gap the widest?
2 Between which two adjacent quintiles is the income gap the narrowest?
3 Approximately, what is the ratio of the bottom quintile's *original income* to that in the top quintile?
4 Approximately, what is the ratio of the bottom quintile's *final income* to that in the top quintile?
5 What do the last two answers tell you about the impact of the tax/welfare system on the distribution of income? Does it make it more or less egalitarian?
6 One of the household types more likely to be found in the original-income section in the bottom quintile is that of pensioner households. Suggest two other such types.
7 With reference to the comments above on progressive and regressive taxation, (a) calculate whether the bottom quintile loses more from direct taxes or from indirect taxes, and (b) do the same for the top quintile.

When making comparisons over time, a decision always has to be made as to what period should be included, and thus what starting point should be chosen. Sometimes, this choice may be dictated by methodological constraints. For example, data may not be available beyond a certain point, or it may have been collected in such a different way as to make comparisons invalid.

Sometimes, however, a date is chosen because it has some sociological, or perhaps political, significance. In this approach, a particular event or period is seen as watershed, a time when social change began to accelerate or shifted in a new direction. The Second World War is considered to be one such watershed ('before the War … ' is often said). So too is 1979. This is the year in which the Conservatives returned to government under Margaret Thatcher. This government implemented a range of policies which were often sharply different, not just from those of previous Labour governments but also from those of postwar Conservative governments.

To choose 1979 as a starting point for comparisons, therefore, has a real sociological validity because it seeks to assess the social impact of a new political regime, one that was to last for nearly two decades. Having said this, there may be a political motive in choosing this date as well. Those sociologists of a Left persuasion may choose 1979 as a starting point for statistical comparison because it enables them to make a political point.

THE 1979 ELECTION OF MARGARET THATCHER AS BRITAIN'S PRIME MINISTER MARKED A POLITICAL AND
SOCIOLOGICAL TURNING POINT AS THE POLICIES OF HER GOVERNMENT WERE OFTEN SHARPLY DIFFERENT
FROM THOSE OF PREVIOUS LABOUR AND POSTWAR CONSERVATIVE GOVERNMENTS.

The Second World War and its aftermath: more equality

There is general acceptance of the view that income inequality narrowed during
the post-Second World War economic boom. This is put down to such factors as
full employment, the influence of trade unions on boosting manual workers'
wages and some redistributive effects of the tax/benefit system. However, this
gentle equalising still left the pattern of incomes very unequal.

The Conservative Government, 1979–97: more inequality, and then less?

The trend towards greater income equality ended in the 1970s. Under the
Conservative Governments of Mrs Thatcher, it became more unequal, so much so
in fact that one report suggested that it had become the most unequal since
records began at the end of the last century (*The Guardian*, March 1994). Evidence
of widening income inequality came in an international research report by the
Organisation of Economic Co-operation and Development. This measured
inequality levels in many industrialised countries from 1979 to 1995. It did so by
comparing the trends in the ratios of the top 10 per cent of male earners to those
of the bottom 10 per cent of male earners. Clearly, the higher the number, the

greater the inequality. In this period, the UK number rose faster than in any other country except for the USA. In 1979, the ratio in Britain was under 2.5, but by 1995, it was around 3.3. Through this change, Britain overtook countries like Australia and Japan in terms of income inequality. Of the industrialised countries, only New Zealand saw inequality grow more over the 1980s than it did in Britain (*The Guardian*, 28 April 1997).

One justification for choosing 1979 as a key watershed as outlined above is the way that tax policy was used as a vehicle for redistributing income – in favour of the well off. One commentator noted that:

> *If the share in post-tax income of the richest 20% were dropped back to where it was in 1979, they would forfeit £18.5 billion …*
>
> Wells, *The Guardian*, 7 April 1997

This shift in favour of the well off did not come evenly throughout the period. There were certain times when annual tax changes in the Budget brought massive advantage to the higher-income groups. One such time, referred to above, was when the rate of VAT was increased from 8 per cent to 15 per cent in one step. As has been seen, VAT is a regressive tax, taking proportionately more from low-income groups than from others. This example shows how important it is that discussions of the tax burden do not concentrate exclusively on income tax. One occasion when income tax changes massively redistributed income in favour of the well off was in 1988 when (as already mentioned) the top rate of income tax was reduced from 60 per cent to 40 per cent.

Post-Thatcher 1: the Major years

The previous trend towards greater equality returned shortly after John Major replaced Mrs Thatcher as Prime Minister (The Family Expenditure Survey, *The Guardian*, 17 October 1997). This was not wholly, or perhaps even mainly, a direct result of his new policies, though there were some of relevance. Several explanations have been put forward for this trend reversal. One is that there was a halt in the rise of the number of workless households, the first since 1979. Another was the growing impact of private and occupational pension schemes on the incomes of the retired. Finally, there were some tax cuts in the pre-1997 election period which slightly favoured the less well off.

Post-Thatcher 2: 1997 and after – the Labour Government

The Labour Party has traditionally had an image of being in favour of higher public spending, particularly on health and welfare, and higher levels of income tax, particularly on top earners. These policies were part of the redistributive and egalitarian ideology associated with social democracy and socialism. What characterised the Party's campaign to win the 1997 General Election was its commitment to keeping to the previous Conservative Government's tax and spending plans. This meant that the use of taxation to shift resources from the rich to the poor seemed unlikely. Any spending on the welfare of the poor or socially excluded would have to come from economic growth.

With this in mind, it is worth noting the analysis of the first three Labour Budgets. The top-income decile lost out, though only a little, whilst the bottom three gained most, though not hugely (Institute of Fiscal Studies, cited in *The Observer*, 14 March 1999).

INCOME INEQUALITIES

This issue is directly addressed elsewhere in relation to the specific issues of old age, unemployment and the labour market, where explanations of the inequalities are examined. The present section is more descriptive and seeks to give a general overview of the connection between income distribution and the main social stratification variables, especially those of class, gender and ethnicity.

CLASS INEQUALITIES

Wages and salaries in the 1980s
There is clear evidence that the class income gap widened in the 1980s. It was widened by changes at both ends of the income hierarchy.

From the lower-income end, inequality was widened by factors like increases in unemployment (though this fluctuated), increases in the numbers of workers in low-paid jobs, and cuts in the real level of some social security benefits. One illustration of the point about low wages is found in Department of Employment figures on the number of full-time workers earning less than two-thirds of the average gross earnings for full-timers. The number in this category rose by nearly 800,000 to 4,680,000 from 1978 to 1992 (*The Guardian*, 26 August 1992).

From the top end, inequality was widened by several factors. One was the cuts in tax rates on the well off. Another was the government-encouraged culture of higher rewards for talent and responsibility, for people whom the government called 'wealth creators' and 'risk takers'. An example of this was the very large pay rises awarded to the top managers of utilities, like gas and water, after they were privatised in the 1980s and 1990s.

Sometimes, statistical categories like the quintiles used in the *Social Trends* table above (see Table 2) are too large and too anonymous to give a sense of what the pay gap means to particular groups of employees. The following comparison should give a better feel for this. In 1998, the median remuneration of the chief executives of the top 100 companies quoted on the *Financial Times* stock exchange index, was £570,500 (*The Guardian*, 17 April 1998). One month later, the government announced the level of the first ever, national minimum wage in Britain. It was to be set at £3.60 per hour for those over 21 and £3.20 for 18-21 year olds. The government's Office for National Statistics estimated that the numbers earning below these levels were at least 2 million and 275,000 respectively.

Labour-market participation – risk and insecurity

Sociology seems to be in a permanent debate about the definition, categorisation and importance of class. Traditionally, the manual/non-manual work distinction was used as the main measure of class, and inequalities based on this were seen as amongst the most significant in society. This division still has analytic value. For example, the Low Pay Unit has shown that in 1997, the poorest manual workers were worse off compared to the average than at any other time since records began in 1886 (*The Independent*, 16 October 1998).

However, there have been many challenges to this approach, one of which is particularly relevant to the measurement of income inequalities. This is the one proposed by the economics journalist Will Hutton. The key variable in his approach is not type of labour (mental or physical) but degrees of labour-market

Table 3: *Hutton's '30/30/40 society'*	
THE ADVANTAGED 40%	PERCENTAGE OF ADULTS 16–59/64
Full-time for two years or more (excluding those below 50% of median earnings)	31%
Full-time self-employed for two years or more	5%
Part-time for five years or more	6%
THE NEWLY INSECURE 30%	
Full-time employees for less than two years (as well as those in employment for longer but on less than half median earnings)	12%
Full-time self-employed for up to two years (plus part-time self-employed)	5%
Part-time for less than five years	7%
Temporary	4%
THE DISADVANTAGED 30%	
Unemployed	8%
Inactive	21%
On training programmes (plus unpaid family workers)	1%

Source: W. Hutton, *The Guardian*, 30 October 1995.

involvement and security. On this basis, Hutton (1995) identifies what he calls the '30/30/40 society'. The constituent groups of this division are shown in Table 3.

Of course, these rough statistical divisions are not set in stone – unemployment can rise or fall quite quickly for example – but they do suggest the scale of new socio-economic divisions in British society. What is not indicated by the categories alone is their full social significance.

Whilst the top 40 per cent are well off in many respects, there is probably less security within this group than at any other time over the previous half century. In any case, the size of this group is shrinking by about 1 per cent per year.

The inequalities experienced by the bottom 30 per cent are often associated with increased marginalisation and the exclusion of particular social groups. This might involve difficulty in obtaining a mortgage or decent rented accommodation, perhaps even complete homelessness. Shelter reports that part-time workers and the self-employed are three times more likely than the permanently employed to get into mortgage arrears and lose their homes (*The Guardian*, 16 November 1998). This could, in turn, involve difficulty in registering to vote, or perhaps even an unwillingness to. There is also likely to be less than full access to the provisions of state health and welfare, such as not being registered with a doctor or dentist. There may additionally be difficulties in sustaining a stable family life, and other personal problems as well.

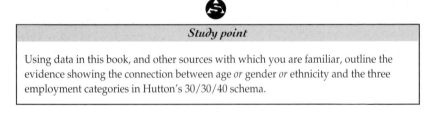

Study point

Using data in this book, and other sources with which you are familiar, outline the evidence showing the connection between age *or* gender *or* ethnicity and the three employment categories in Hutton's 30/30/40 schema.

Points of evaluation – an exercise in understanding validity

One of the most important concepts in the evaluation of research is that of *validity*. In sociology, there is both a general and a specific meaning to this concept. At the general level, research is invalid if it is biased, based on data which is unreliable or samples which are used for generalisation but which are not representative of the population from which they were drawn. At a more specific level, validity refers to the question of whether or not a measure actually measures what it is being used to measure. It is often associated with the research task known as the *operationalisation of concepts*. This refers to the process by which a complex idea is converted into a more practical measure, or set of measures, that can be applied more easily in research.

In Hutton's 30/30/40 schema (1995), one key concept that is operationalised is that of employment 'risk' and this is used as a measure of socio-economic disadvantage. Risk is measured through employment type.

The following are all used as indicators of disadvantage: self-employment, part-time employment, short duration of employment (ie under two years), and temporary employment. They may be fairly sound indicators of such. However, even very good indicators are not perfect.

Study point

For each indicator of disadvantage or insecurity in the boxed list above, suggest one way in which the employment category may not necessarily be a necessary indicator of economic disadvantage.

GENDER INEQUALITIES

There has been some change in the relative earnings of women and men since the 1970s sex-equality laws came into force. In 1970, the average weekly pay of women was just 55 per cent of men's (Alcock, 1996). By 1991, it was 71 per cent (Abercrombie and Warde, 1994). However, figures show that the gap widened in 1997 for the first time in 10 years (Office of National Statistics, 1998). This was partly because female-dominated professions have had their pay kept down more than some other occupational groups – an indirect form of gender discrimination, says a pay expert from the business organisation, Income Data Services (*The Guardian*, 16 October 1998).

Study point

What female-dominated professions do you think are being referred to here?

Rather than look at the gender pay gap in terms of overall averages, however, it is more illuminating here to analyse it in terms of the occupational categories associated with social class. This is because there are times when it makes sense to study women as a singular gender category and there are times when it is necessary to take other factors into account, such as occupational class.

The New Earnings Survey gives details of *average* pay levels according to gender, region and category of employment (ie manual or non-manual). What this shows is that full-time, male non-manual workers earned significantly more than full-time, male manual workers – anything from 30 per cent to around 60 per cent more. This was true regardless of region. The same non-manual/manual inequality existed for women as well, though with different percentage gaps. These patterns show the significance of class factors in employment incomes.

However, a different pattern emerges when women and men are compared to each other. Excluding the south-east of England, where average incomes are generally higher and substantially higher for non-manual employment, the following gender pattern emerges. In every region, the average incomes of *male manual* workers is higher than those of *female non-manual* workers (HMSO, 1990, as reproduced in Kirby et al., 1993). The explanation for this is partly to be found in the kinds of non-manual employment in which women and men are generally located. Women are much more concentrated in the clerical and lower-professional types of employment, whereas men are found more in the higher professions and management. Even where women and men are in the same broad occupational groupings, men may be further up the career ladder than women.

It is important to note, as well, that these are *average* income figures only: it is obvious that many female non-manual workers earn more than many male manual workers, and so on.

ETHNIC INEQUALITIES

In all discussions of ethnicity, it is absolutely vital that the diversity of Britain's minority ethnic population be recognised. This diversity encompasses many elements, but some of them are different expressions of the same underlying differences. They include:

1 The main periods of immigration and settlement in Britain
2 national backgrounds
3 previous economic circumstances
4 cultures and religions
5 first languages
6 class locations
7 educational achievement levels.

Recognising the importance of this diversity and considering each group in terms of its distinctiveness is known as *the principle of disaggregation*.

Data on income inequality according to ethnic background is collected much less frequently than data on employment and unemployment levels according to ethnicity. In practice, income inequalities according to ethnicity are often derived from these other data on unemployment rates and job levels. However, the previous section on gender showed that moving from data on job levels of men and women to assumptions about their income levels is not always valid.

Data from the 1982 PSI survey shows that there are ethnic-specific factors which also make this move problematic. One example is enough to indicate what this means. In 1982, the median weekly earnings of white males in the professional, managerial and employer category was £184.70; for Asians and West Indians in the same occupational group, the figure was £151.80.

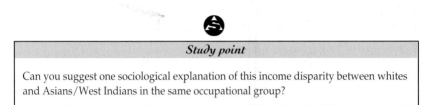

Study point
Can you suggest one sociological explanation of this income disparity between whites and Asians/West Indians in the same occupational group?

The 1982 PSI survey – some points of interpretation and evaluation

There are two general points to note when considering the 1982 PSI data above on ethnicity and earnings, apart from the fact that is it based on research from nearly 20 years ago.

One relates to the fact that these figures refer only to male earnings. Inequalities in income and job levels between ethnic groups are greater among men than among women. This is because women are already disadvantaged, regardless of their ethnic identity.

The other is that the income variations between ethnic minority groups are often as significant as the income variations between ethnic minority groups as a whole and the ethnic majority population (ie whites). This illustrates the point that it does not make sociological sense to operate as if all ethnic minorities were more or less one homogenous group.

These two points are fully illustrated by Table 4 (see p 24).

Sport, meritocracy and racism – a case study

A more recent example of the problem referred to above of relating job level to income is to be found in the more specific area of professional football. A study of footballers' pay was carried out by **Stefan Szymanksi** for the Institute of Public Policy Research (IPPR) (reported in *The Observer Business Section*, 6 April 1997). It was based on a representative sample of 39 clubs between 1978 and 1993 and looked at the proportion of black players in teams, the success of the teams and their wage bills. The basic conclusion was that the wages bills of successful teams with above-average numbers of black players were lower than those of similarly successful teams with fewer black players. As with all research, these findings have to be considered critically before they are accepted. *The Observer* quotes two commentators' views on this research:

Points of evaluation

- *Evaluation 1: ideological*. This comes from a well-known footballers' agent, **Eric Hall**. He is simply quoted as re-affirming the ideology of meritocracy, saying that:

The guy sounds like a monster schmuck ... . It doesn't matter whether you are black, white, Italian, French or German, if you are good enough you will get the money.

The lack of evidence from him in the article does not mean that he could not have cited some had he had space there to do so.

- *Evaluation 2: sociological*. This comes from Professor **John Williams** of The Leicester University Centre for Football Research. He indicates no surprise at the apparent existence of racism in football, but does suggest an *additional* possible explanation for the earnings disparity referred to: age. It may be that the recent growth in the number of black players has resulted in the average age of black and white players being different. As younger players are generally paid less than older ones, this could be a factor that needs to be put into the equation.

Whilst this research, being a kind of case study, cannot readily be generalised from, it is a valuable illustration of the ways in which racial discrimination can operate in specific areas, sometimes in quite hidden ways.

Another such example can be seen in the field of small-business finance, in research for the Forum of Private Business carried out by **Binks** and **Ennew** of Nottingham University. A survey of 10,000 small businesses showed that non-white business owners were treated differently from white ones (*The Guardian*, 21 September 1998). Non-white business owners found it harder to obtain bank loans, had to provide more collateral to get them, and paid higher rates of interest on them.

NB: see again the sections on unemployment, old age and poverty for further discussion of ethnic inequalities in income. See also the section on explanations of inequality later in this chapter. (See pp 24–26.)

REGIONAL INEQUALITIES

Regional inequalities sometimes get confused with class inequalities because the north of England and parts of Scotland and Wales have had more industrial/manual employment than the south of England. This short section here, though only concerned with income differences, may throw a little light on the debate over whether or not Britain has a north–south divide. Although this is more than just a question of income distribution, it is relevant to the debate.

- There are large regional variations in average incomes from employment, and from other sources. By far the highest paid region is the South-east (New Earnings Survey 1990, as reproduced in Kirby et al. 1993).
- In regional terms, however, there appears to be not so much a north–south divide in incomes as a London/South-east and the-rest division.
- The divide seems to be widening. According to a report for the Low Pay Network, in 1997, average Greater London earnings were £455 per week, over £140 more than the average in the lowest region, Wales. This considerably reflects the very specific labour market in London, with the many financial, media and other corporate institutions located there. It does need to be remembered that the costs of housing in London are much greater than in most other areas of Britain, and that income differentials do not automatically translate into standard-of-living differentials of the same order. Neither can standards of living be translated directly into quality of life.
- Within all regions, however, there are significant inequalities in incomes and living standards. Indeed, London, in the South-east, has some of the poorest people in the whole of Britain.

AGE INEQUALITIES

The situation of older workers is explored more fully in the section on premature exit from the labour market in Chapter 4 (see p 78).

As regards the young, there has been a massive decline in their labour-market participation, partly because of the growth in unemployment and partly because of a huge increase in staying on in education beyond the minimum school-leaving age. In 1963, the Robbins Report recommended the doubling of the percentage of the relevant age group going on to higher education by 1980; an increase from 8 per cent to 17 per cent was envisaged (Corbett, 1973). By the time Sir Ron Dearing had finished his investigation into higher education in 1997, this figure had reached 30 per cent. In 40 years, higher education has moved from an elite to a mass experience.

With respect to the earnings of the young employed, it is worth noting that the decline of unskilled manual work is likely to depress their average earnings. This is because it is in this kind of work that young people can reach their maximum earnings potential much earlier. From the late 1970s to the early 1990s, the average earnings of 18–20 year olds did fall from 61 per cent to 53 per cent of overall average earnings (Popple and Kirby, 1997). Despite this, there has been, 'a sizeable shift in the composition of low-paid men away from young people to those aged 25–49.' (Pile and O'Donnell, 1997). Many of these men will be part, or sole, family breadwinners, and their low pay will have direct consequences for the numbers of children living in poverty.

It should be remembered that young people's incomes have also been hit by changes to benefits, particularly the abolition of Income Support for under-18s and significant cuts in housing benefit provision. There has also been the switch from student grants to loans as well as the imposition of university tuition fees.

EXPLANATIONS OF INCOME INEQUALITIES

This section offers explanations for some of the income inequalities above. It is not concerned with general theories of inequality or social stratification. These issues are important, but the main concern here is an exploration of those mechanisms that have had a direct influence on patterns of income distribution in recent decades.

Most of this account will concentrate on the public sphere of the labour market, state regulation and so on. It will be clear to all students of sociology, however, that income differences between women and men are often rooted in, or reinforced by, the influence of the private, domestic sphere – the family. It is inequalities in this sphere that often limit women to part-time employment, at least for a while; and to jobs rather than careers; and imposes limits on career trajectories through limits on both mobility and time investment in promotion (working late, conferences, etc), and through 'career breaks'.

The main focus in this section is on incomes from employment. The reason for this is that incomes from welfare sources are dealt with in the poverty and welfare chapters, as well as in the chapter on old age. In understanding income inequalities, there also needs to be some recognition of those who obtain their income from property, from the ownership of wealth. Data on the distribution of wealth is to be found in the next chapter (see pp 43–46).

1 The labour market – patterns and changes
Dual-labour-market theory
One theory of labour-market inequality in countries like Britain and the USA suggests that the terms under which people sell their labour have been changing over recent decades. This is because the labour market has become divided in two: *primary* and *secondary* labour markets.

The primary labour market is the employment sector where core workers, central to the production process, are highly trained and both difficult and expensive to replace. It is often located in those industries, or sectors of industries, which make use of advanced technology. For these reasons, not only do these workers have relatively high incomes, but their jobs have high security and prospects. The so-called fringe benefits of employment are more attractive also: pension schemes, holiday entitlement, private health insurance and so on.

In contrast to this, the secondary labour market is more often found in industries which are less advanced technologically and which need a large number of relatively unskilled workers. In all industrial sectors, however, there may be workers whose tasks require little training and who can be fairly readily replaced. Employers have no need to pay high wages, salaries or additional benefits to attract or retain these workers. The pattern of employment here is more likely to be part-time, temporary and/or casual, rather than full-time and permanent. Trade unions here are less likely to be recognised by employers, reinforcing the weakness of workers in the labour market.

If it remained in this form, the theory would be a purely structural one, but it does not. It is also concerned with the way certain groups become concentrated in each of the sectors. In particular, it looks at how women and ethnic minorities seem more likely to be found in the secondary labour market. This is why the theory is often found in textbook chapters dealing with women's disadvantage in employment, or in some accounts of 'underclass' theory. The quotation marks here are simply intended to indicate that 'underclass' is a highly controversial concept, one that has been used in so many conflicting ways as to be of doubtful sociological value now.

It is worth noting at this point that women's labour-market participation is now higher than at any time this century, wartime excepted.

Study point

Does the dual-labour-market theory seem to be based more on the theories of Marx or more on those of Weber? Give reasons for your answer.

Gender and occupational segregation
Another set of concepts concerned with the gendering of the labour market is that of *vertical* and *horizontal segregation*. Vertical segregation refers to the situation of one gender being located higher up the occupational hierarchy than the other; in practice, this means that men usually have the higher jobs. Horizontal segregation refers to the fact that, even when women and men are employed at similar levels, they are often in different occupational or industrial sectors. There are many occupational and industrial sectors that are predominantly female. This means that the low pay of women in these sectors cannot readily be improved through equal-pay legislation because they are not being paid less than men at the same place of work.

Activity

It is an interesting exercise to explore the degree of occupational segregation in your school or college, or place of employment for that matter.

The research can be carried out by observation and just a little questioning in small organisations, but larger organisations might require more systematic investigation. One student at my college used the internal college telephone directory to match names to job levels and areas. She did find problems in converting some names into gender categories and in working out what some job titles really meant in hierarchical terms. Some college staff were not listed in the directory either, such as canteen staff and cleaners.

The research should consider data on the overall ratio of female to male employers, perhaps taking into account full- and part-time differences, as well as the patterns of vertical and horizontal segregation themselves.

Ethnicity and the occupational structure

Just as gender income inequalities partly stem from differences in employment patterns, so too do many of the income inequalities along ethnic lines.

Table 4 is adapted from the latest of the more or less decennial surveys (ie every 10 years) of Britain's ethnic minority population by the Policy Studies Institute. This one is based on Labour Force Surveys in 1988, 1989 and 1990. It shows job levels according to ethnicity and gender, and it can be used as an indicator of income inequalities along these lines. As the comments above show, using the table in this way is likely to underestimate the degree of ethnic income inequality.

Table 4: *Job levels according to ethnicity and gender (%)*							
ETHNIC GROUP	OCCUPATIONAL CATEGORY						
	MALES				FEMALES		
	I	II	III	IV	I	II	III	IV
All Origins	27	20	32	19	11	55	5	29
White	27	20	33	19	11	56	5	29
Total Ethnic Minority	21	22	28	28	9	53	5	32
Afro-Caribbean	12	19	39	29	8	54	4	34
African Asian	27	30	26	16	7	58	9	26
Indian	25	18	29	28	10	47	5	38
Pakistani	12	16	34	37	4	42	7	47
Bangladeshi	12	14	5	70	*	*	*	*
Chinese	30	19	10	40	16	53	2	29
African	21	34	20	22	11	47	6	36
Other/Mixed	30	31	18	18	12	63	3	22

SOURCE: POLICY STUDIES INSTITUTE, 1988, 1989 AND 1990.

* = sample size too small

Notes and comments on Table 4 are as follows:

1 *Occupational categories.* In the table, the occupational-category numbers refer to the following:

I   = professional, managerial, employer
II = other non-manual
III = skilled manual and foreman
IV = semi & unskilled manual.

2 *The data varies from the original in a number of ways:*

a Originally, data for the professional, managerial, employer category were broken down into three separate subcategories as well as in aggregated form. These subcategories distinguished managers and employers from employed professionals and had separate figures for managers and employers according to the size of the establishments they owned or managed. One point of interest here is that whites had the highest percentage in the 'large' establishments category, but not in the 'small' establishments category.

b Data for the other non-manual category were not subdivided into subcategories. This is a pity because about half of the employed women in all the ethnic groupings (except Bangladeshi) were in this group. However, the data in the table do not enable us to see at what level, within this broad category, they were all employed.

c The figures for semi-skilled and unskilled manual were originally given separately. The decision to amalgamate them here was taken for two reasons. Firstly, it condensed and simplified a very large table. Secondly, the life chances of these two groups have enough in common for this amalgamation to be reasonably justifiable in sociological terms.

3 *Group sizes and their significance.*

a The fact that these figures are percentages needs to be emphasised. The actual number of people from the various ethnic groupings in the occupational categories indicated depends on the size of that ethnic group in Britain and not just on the percentages listed.

b Following on from this, the similarity between the White category and the All Origins category needs to be noted. This stems from the fact that whites constitute about 94 per cent of the entire population.

4 *Interpreting the tables – patterns of advantage and disadvantage.*

a One way of looking at the patterns of advantage and disadvantage is to consider the proportions of the various ethnic groupings which are located in the top occupational category, that of employers, managers and professionals. The problematic validity of reading off income directly from job level has been noted. Notwithstanding this, it seems reasonable to argue that the larger the proportion of an ethnic group that is in one of these top jobs, the larger the proportion of that group will be on high incomes. On this basis, the ethnic groups most likely to be in the highest paid jobs are, for men, Chinese, whites and African Asians, and, for women, Chinese, whites, Africans and Indians.

b The average incomes of a whole group and overall calculations of advantage and disadvantage depend on more than the percentage in top jobs. The distribution across the whole occupational structure needs to be considered, perhaps especially the percentage in the bottom category. This takes us towards the specific issue of poverty that will be discussed separately. However, the significant over representation of some ethnic groups in the semi-skilled and unskilled category needs to be noted. One such overrepresented group, interestingly, is the Chinese, at least Chinese men. This shows that the danger of overgeneralisation about ethnic minority groups – or even of stereotyping them – does not disappear once they have been disaggregated. Chinese men seem to be simultaneously advantaged and disadvantaged. In short, there is class variation within groups as well as between them.

5 *Ethnicity, class and gender.*
   a The class variation within ethnic groups, just like those between them, is considerably greater for men than for women.
   b Perhaps the most striking illustration of this is to be found in the percentages in the top occupational category. For men, the lowest proportion in this category is 12 per cent (Pakistani, Bangladeshi, Afro-Caribbean); only Chinese women exceed this figure. More significant, perhaps, is the *variation* in the representation of men and women in the top occupational category, according to different ethnic backgrounds. Thus, for women, all but two of the ethnic groups have between 7 per cent and 11 per cent of their members in this category, though Bangladeshis are excluded from this calculation. For men, the distribution is from 12 per cent to 30 per cent, with three specific groups at or near either extreme.
   c In short, women were generally less likely to reach the top occupational group than men, regardless of ethnic background.

The decline of the full-time, permanent job

Work is changing. There are fewer manual workers in employment as industries like mining and manufacturing decline. In addition, however, there are changes in what it means to have a job. In the 30 or so years of the postwar economic boom, paid work generally had the following features: permanent rather than temporary; mostly full-time; relatively little self-employment; and a job for most who sought one (with significant regional exceptions).

In the 20 or more years since the end of this boom, in the 1970s, things have changed considerably. Some of these changes are associated with the sectoral shifts described in dual-labour-market theory. Some are more specifically to do with employers' strategies of imposing 'flexibility' on their decreasingly unionised workforces. The following changes have been recorded.

Between 1984 and 1994, the number of:

- self-employed workers grew by 23 per cent
- part-time employees grew by 19 per cent
- temporary workers grew by 6 per cent
- full-time employees grew by just 0.1 per cent
- permanent workers fell by 8 per cent

SOURCE: OPPENHEIM AND HARKER, (1996).

These figures probably understate the changes which have occurred, most notably in the level of job security. See Hutton's analysis above on pp. 15–16.

In addition, there is the probable growth of the 'black economy'. This refers to undeclared paid work. Because it is undeclared, there are no accurate records of its extent or of who is most involved in it. Nonetheless, there is some research upon which to draw. A report for the EU Social Affairs Commission estimated that between 7 per cent and 13 per cent of Britain's gross domestic product is in the 'black economy'. Some of the jobs here are being done by those registered as unemployed, by students, by the early retired and by housewives. However, it is estimated that most of the jobs in the 'black economy' are carried out by those already in regular employment. If this is so, it adds to the contrast between the so-called 'work-rich' and 'work-poor' households.

A second factor to consider is that, because this is work on which no direct taxation is paid, there is a higher tax burden on workers in the formal economy who are paying income tax. (See pp. 105–107.)

Interventionism and regulation of the labour market
Market forces alone do not determine the price of labour or the contracts and conditions of employment of those selling their labour. Workers themselves seek to use their collective power as members of trade unions or professional associations to push market forces in their favour. Sometimes, governments, perhaps under pressure from trade unions, seek to regulate the labour market by protective legislation of various kinds.

Trade unions and professional associations
Trade unionism developed in the nineteenth century as a way in which workers could organise themselves collectively to overcome their relative weakness as individuals in seeking to influence their wages and conditions of employment. Initially, they were outlawed and opposed strongly by the state and by employers, but gradually their legal status was accepted, and membership grew. Membership peaked at the end of the 1970s, as did union bargaining power and political influence.

After 1979, the new Conservative Government sought to weaken trade unionism. A Marxist view would be that the government was engaged in a kind of class warfare, siding with the capitalists to weaken the organised working class. The government certainly made no secret of its view that it thought that trade unions were too powerful, sometimes justifying this by reference to its free-market ideology. Trade unions were seen as interfering with the free movement of market forces and, in particular, as preventing wages from rising or falling according to the forces of supply and demand. Wages kept 'artificially' high would be too expensive for employers, and higher unemployment was said to result. Accordingly, the government acted to weaken trade unions by three main measures. There was a series of laws restricting trade unions' freedom to act effectively to protect their members. There was a major confrontation in 1984/85 with one of the strongest unions, that of the miners, the aim being to impose a significant and symbolic defeat on them. There was also the apparently deliberate use of increased unemployment to weaken unions' bargaining power and reduce their membership.

The impact of these and other changes on trade union membership was quite dramatic, as the trend briefly described here shows. Membership fell from just over 12 million members in 1979 to less than 7 million after 18 years of Conservative Government. The 1999 Labour Force Survey shows a slight rise in union membership, the first for 19 years. Professional associations generally have a much higher degree of control, even a monopoly, over their labour-market situation than any unionised workers. With the supply of labour artificially scarce, the price of labour is accordingly artificially high (Esland, 1976). The Conservatives did make some attempts to weaken the power of some professional groups to make them more open to competition and market forces, such as scrapping the solicitors' monopoly right to property conveyancing. However, their situation was not dramatically weakened in the way that that of the organised working class was.

Wages protection – regulation and deregulation
In the 1980s and early 1990s, the dominant government ideology was that of non-intervention in the economy and of deregulation. Accordingly, minimum-wage protection for young people, and then for adults, in low-wage industries was scrapped.

In June 1998, the Labour Government, which had taken office in 1997, introduced a minimum wage that covered all workers. The level was set quite low, and there was a lower rate for young workers, but it was still high enough to help protect 2 million employees. (*The Guardian*, 19 June 1998).

The state and anti-discrimination legislation
- *The 1970s sex-equality legislation.* The earnings of women relative to those of men have to be understood against the background of government policy which officially claims to seek equality of treatment for women and men in the labour market. The most important contribution to this policy came in the

1970s. Three Acts of Parliament, all passed or coming into force in 1975, made some attempt to tackle the practices of paying women less than men for the same work and of giving men preference over women in employment and promotion. Full equality has not come since then. There are two main reasons for this. First, there were flaws and loopholes in the legislation, some of which have been remedied since. Second, as has already been seen, there are other sources of gender inequality in pay and employment than those caused by discrimination.

- *Race-relations legislation.* Just as with gender, so too with 'race': officially, there is a commitment to equal treatment of whites and ethnic minorities in employment. Again, however, as with gender, the legislation has not brought about full equality. In the case of race-discrimination legislation, the first law was introduced in the 1960s and tightened up in 1976. There are three key provisions that need to be noted here. The law forbids employers from treating people less favourably on grounds of race. It also forbids them from applying conditions to employment that indirectly discriminate against people on the same grounds. Finally, it also makes it an offence to victimise someone who makes a complaint about discrimination.

- *Disability Legislation.* In 1996, the Conservative Government brought in a Disability Discrimination Act. It made it unlawful for an employer of more than 20 people to treat disabled people less favourably, unless 'good reason' can be shown. However, the Act was not strong enough for many in the alliance of disability campaigning groups. Labour has proposed a stronger Disability Commission starting in 2000.

- *Age Discrimination.* In 1998, the government announced a draft voluntary code of practice for employers to attempt to reduce age discrimination in employment. 'Third age' pressure groups would prefer to have legislation to outlaw age discrimination in the way that race and sex discrimination are outlawed.

The Role of Europe in influencing labour-market regulation

On a number of occasions over the past two decades, Britain's laws on workers' rights or social security have been declared out of keeping with her obligations as a member of the European Community/Union. Many of these obligations have been concerned with equal treatment of men and women. Sometimes, a concern with the lack of rights of part-time workers, so many of whom are women, has been expressed. One development here came in April 1998 when the British Government published regulations outlining how it was to comply with the European Working Time Directive. One major element to this was the extension of paid holiday entitlement to the 1 in 8 proportion of the British workforce not previously entitled to such. Most of these 2.5 million workers to benefit are women.

The privatisation of public utilities and the contracting-out of many services in the public sector often worsened the employment situation of those already employed in these services. This process also came under the spotlight of European law. In 1997, the High Court in London applied a 1977 European

Community directive to the way that the Conservative Government had deliberately failed to protect workers' wages and conditions in the process of contracting-out jobs to the private sector. Thousands of workers stood to gain large sums in compensation (Pile and O'Donnell, 1997).

UNEMPLOYMENT — A CASE STUDY IN INCOME LOSS

Introduction

Participation in the labour market is a major determinant of income and the need for welfare. This is clearly demonstrated by the cases of those who are not in employment. The next chapter is devoted to those who have retired and permanently left the labour market. This chapter looks at unemployment. This may not affect as many people for so long as does retirement, but it does affect millions of people at some stage in their lifetimes, sometimes for many years. It therefore justifies some separate discussion, though a briefer one than retirement.

UNEMPLOYMENT STATISTICS

Unemployment statistics are published monthly by the Department for Education and Employment. As every student of A level sociology will know, there is a general debate about the use of statistics in sociology and a more specific one about the value of official statistics to the sociologist. Both debates are best left to books dealing explicitly with theory and methods (see, for example, Barrat and Cole, 1991, or Slattery, 1986). Some discussion of the official statistics of unemployment is necessary, however.

Points of evaluation
Some of the problems confronting the sociologist wishing to use these statistics are probably generic, that is they relate to the general problem of defining and measuring unemployment. Others come from the increased politicisation of these, and other, official statistics over the 1980s and 1990s. Over 20 times, the Conservative Governments of this period changed the way unemployment was measured. There were two related themes to many of these changes:

1 There were changes to entitlement to unemployment benefit. Certain groups were excluded from this altogether; for example, in 1988, 16/17-year-old jobless school leavers had benefit entitlement withdrawn. A separate change was that all claimants had to pass a stiffer test to prove that they were 'genuinely seeking work'. Jobseeker's Allowance replaced Unemployment

Benefit in October 1996. There were two important elements to this change worth noting here. First, stricter rules regarding proof of 'actively seeking work' were introduced. Second, there was a reduction in the period that claimants could get benefit without undergoing a means test, from 12 to 6 months.

2 Only people actually in receipt of unemployment benefit were counted as unemployed. Those without jobs but who could not claim, or qualify for, this benefit, were lost from the count.

Each of these, and most of the other, changes to the method of counting led to a fall in the recorded rate of unemployment. Critics also argued that the operation of the 'genuinely-seeking-work test' was leading to genuine claimants' being unfairly pressured to come off the unemployment register. Interestingly, the two changes associated with the Jobseeker's Allowance just mentioned reduced the claimant count of unemployed by up to 200,000 (Office of National Statistics, *The Guardian*, 10 April 1998).

All these changes led to huge disillusionment with the government's unemployment statistics; by the end of the period in question, 97 per cent of the population did not trust them (reported in *The Observer Business Section*, 15 February 1998). Even if all the changes had been to make the measure more 'accurate', it would still be impossible to make comparisons over time. This is because the rates would have been calculated in different ways. Put in a nutshell, falls in the recorded rate of unemployment over the 1980s to 1990s do not necessarily indicate falls in the 'real' rate of unemployment. The impact of all the changes can be seen when the February 1998 unemployment rates are compared, using the claimant count, with the pre-1979 measure: the former comes out as 1.38 million and the latter as 2.67 million (*The Guardian*, 4 February 1998).

The Labour Government has attempted to take some of the controversy out of measuring unemployment by introducing a new unemployment measure recognised as valid by the International Labour Organisation. Using the Labour Force Survey of 60,000 households, this counts the unemployed as those actively seeking work and available to start in the next week, even if they are not in receipt of benefit. In February 1998, this measure produced a figure of 1.85 million. There is a wider definition still which includes people who have effectively become economically inactive and have dropped out of the labour market. Many of these are women, but not all. On this definition, there were 4.24 million unemployed. (*The Guardian*, 4 February 1998). It is now easy to see why the term, '"real" rate of unemployment' is so problematic.

This wider measure of unemployment points towards another problem with unemployment statistics, and that concerns what they are sometimes used to measure, or what they might be implied to measure. It might be assumed that a growth in employment is a corollary of a decline in the rate of unemployment and vice versa. The 2 million people without jobs but not recorded as unemployed can be seen as an indicator of a phenomenon that was a product of the mass unemployment and harsher benefits regime of the 1980s. This is the process by which some people without jobs officially 'disappear'; they cease to register as unemployed and become officially economically inactive. For example, a report in 1997 for the Employment Policy Institute and the Prince's Trust estimated that as many as half a million young people between 16 and 24 are actually outside the labour market (*The Guardian*, 6 June 1997).

Study point
Use a dictionary of sociology or some other reference, such as a textbook to look up the concepts of *reliability* and *validity*. Write a paragraph on *each* concept indicating how it can be used to assess the value of official statistics of unemployment.

The partially employed

There is yet another issue to consider, one which is looked at in more detail in the section on the changing nature of work and the labour market. (See pp. 15–16 and 22–23.) In the 1950s and 1960s, and perhaps into the 1970s, a decline in unemployment was another way of saying that there had been a growth not just in employment but also very likely in full-time, permanent employment. However, many of the people now who come off the unemployment register into work have temporary, casual or part-time jobs.

Despite all the problems of reliability and validity concerning the competing unemployment measures, it is still possible to make some fairly definite statements about unemployment patterns and trends.

TRENDS IN UNEMPLOYMENT

The postwar period was quite an exceptional one in terms of the duration of what was called full employment – see the trend shown in Table 5.

Table 5: *Unemployment in Britain (%)*			
	AVERAGE UNEMPLOYMENT	MAXIMUM UNEMPLOYMENT	MINIMUM UNEMPLOYMENT
1921–40	14.0	22.5	10.9
1941–70	1.5	2.4	0.4
1971–80	4.0	5.8	2.3

SOURCE: *OXFORD REVIEW OF ECONOMIC POLICY*, VOL. 1, No. 2 (OUP).

In 1979, Mrs Thatcher's Government explicitly abandoned the postwar consensual commitment to full employment and the average unemployment rate between 1980 and 1985 rose to 11.2 per cent, a rate not seen for half a century.

The early/middle years of the 1990s do seem to have brought a *real* decline in unemployment. By early 1999, unemployment was lower than at any time since 1980. Interestingly, it was falling slower than employment was rising, the latter's rise being a product of the economically inactive re-entering the labour force. It is important to remember that the average number of unemployed in a given year or period is not the same as the actual number of people who will have been unemployed during that period. This is demonstrated by statistics from Job Centre returns in late 1995. These illustrated that, between April 1992 and August 1995, 8.5 million people made an average of two unemployment claims (*The Guardian*, 31 October 1995). This is far in excess of the number unemployed at any one time or the average over that period.

ETHNICITY AND UNEMPLOYMENT

The variation in unemployment by ethnic group is shown in Table 6.

Table 6: *Unemployment rates by ethnic group, 1988–90 (%)*		
ETHNIC GROUP	MEN	WOMEN
White	8	7
Afro-Caribbean	16	13
African Asian	8	10
Indian	11	12
Pakistani	22	25
Bangladeshi	24	*

* = SAMPLE TOO SMALL

SOURCE: JONES, 1993, USING LFS DATA.

⌾

1   How does Table 6 show the importance of disaggregation?
2   How significant is gender as a variable in the differential unemployment rates shown in Table 6?
3   Why do you think that the sample size for Bangladeshi women is too small?

Explanations for the higher unemployment rates for some minority ethnic groups compared to whites vary. A very traditional sociological theory of ethnic difference and inequality comes from the American, **Robert Park**. In the 1920s, he put forward the 'immigrant/host' model of ethnic relations. One aspect of his theory described a race-relations cycle which moved from contact, through competition (eg over jobs) and then accommodation, to assimilation. One of the problems with testing this theory in the British context is that some minority groups have not been in Britain for that long. Nonetheless, there is evidence to suggest that the disadvantage of some minority ethnic groups is not just a matter of what Park called the 'strangeness' to the immigrant, of the ways of the new country. This evidence comes from studies of race discrimination in employment, including among second and third generation immigrants.

Discrimination may be direct or indirect. The former is about individual intention, whereas the latter is where the discrimination is the product of employment or recruitment rules or procedures that, unintentionally or unwittingly, bring about discrimination.

It is very difficult to know how much discrimination of different sorts there is. It cannot be assumed that the entire gap between white and ethnic minority unemployment rates is automatically due to discrimination in the labour market. It may be that the gap is partly a product of differences in educational rates between the various ethnic groups in question, both majority and minority groups. It could be that some of this gap is the product of discrimination in the education system, years before labour-market entry. It may be, however, that inequalities in educational achievement and unemployment rates are partly accountable by factors other than discrimination. One of these relates to the industrial and geographic areas of employment in which many – but not all – ethnic minorities are concentrated. Ethnic minorities have been affected by the general decline of manual work, and more specifically of manufacturing, often in particular regions of the country. Inner city industrial decline has also hit ethnic minority employment prospects (Kumar, 1993).

Comparing the unemployment rates of different ethnic groups and controlling for educational qualification level is an interesting exercise. It points to the extent to which factors other than education affect unemployment rates, and raises questions about the extent of formal meritocracy in British society.

	Table 7: *Highest qualification by ethnic group, 1988–90 (%)* (*selected qualification levels only*)		
ETHNIC GROUP	DEGREE OR EQUIVALENT	O LEVEL OR EQUIVALENT	NONE ACHIEVED
All Origins	3	7	12
White	3	6	12
Total Ethnic Minority	6	13	18
Afro-Caribbean	2	14	20
African Asian	3	9	15
Indian	3	12	16
Pakistani	9	21	24
Bangladeshi	*	*	34
Chinese	5	4	8
African	8	15	22
Other/Mixed	10	12	10

* = SAMPLE SIZE TOO SMALL

SOURCE: JONES, 1993, USING LFS DATA.

Comments and questions on Tables 6 and 7

1 There is a huge amount of information here. The key to statistical interpretation is being selective, looking for main patterns – either striking differences or regular similarities. One important similarity to note in Table 7 is that between the figures for the White and All Origins groups. This is simply an expression of the fact that 94 per cent of the population is White, and consequently, their pattern will significantly determine the overall pattern.

2 Take care not to read too much into differences of one percentage point in unemployment rates. These figures are rounded to whole numbers, and so the real difference between such groups *may* only be 0.2 per cent (eg 2.4 per cent would become 2 per cent whereas 2.6 per cent would become 3 per cent). Another issue to consider is the fact that the statistics come from survey data and there is always a small margin of error, even with large and highly representative samples.

3 Be warned! In Table 6, it is not possible statistically to add these ethnic minorities' unemployment rates together and divide them by the number of groups to create an average for all the groups. This is because the groups have different population sizes, and therefore the unemployment rates of larger groups will have a bigger impact on the overall ethnic minority unemployment rate than the rates of smaller groups.

Study point

1 Table 7 is complicated because it is dealing with two variables that relate to unemployment rates: ethnicity and educational qualifications. Taking just the latter for the moment, look for answers to the following two questions:
  a Is there any ethnic group where there is no correlation between educational qualifications and unemployment rates?
  b How big is the impact that educational qualifications seem to make on unemployment rates?
2 Now consider the following questions more directly concerned with ethnicity and unemployment.
  a Is the rank order of highest to lowest unemployment rates according to qualifications achieved the same, or nearly the same, across all the ethnic groups listed in the table?
  b Where is the ethnic variation in unemployment the widest, among those with high or among those with no educational qualifications? Suggest an explanation for the pattern indicated in your answer.
  c What does the table suggest about the risk of unemployment to people with a degree, regardless of their ethnic background?

AGE AND UNEMPLOYMENT

When considering age and unemployment, it is important to remember the problems with the official statistics. The Conservatives redefined unemployment as being in receipt of benefit instead of registering for work (1982), stopped requiring men over 60 to sign on (1983), and withdrew the entitlement of 16 and 17 year olds to the dole (1988). At both ends of the working-age spectrum, the statistics underestimate the real number of jobless people who want employment.

Unemployment among older workers, including premature exit from the labour market, is dealt with in Chapter 4. Whilst retirement is not the only reason why 40 per cent of the 9.3 million people between 50 and 64 do not have jobs, it is a significant factor (source: Employment Forum on Age, referred to in the *The Guardian*, 17 November 1998).

This section looks primarily at the situation of the young unemployed. Demographic trends have to be taken into account when considering unemployment rates among the young. So too do the changes that have occurred in the patterns of education and training for post-16 year olds. In the 1980s recession, the rise in unemployment generally coincided with a sharp rise in the youth population. Between 1984 and 1996, youth unemployment fell, but so too did the size of the youth population. This meant that the large, half-million drop in the *numbers* of young unemployed (16–24) over that period only produced a small fall in the *percentage* unemployment rate – from 19 per cent to 15 per cent (Convery, 1997).

It is interesting to look back to the period immediately before this one to see how much the career or job paths for 16 year olds have changed since the mid-1970s. In 1975, 3 per cent of 16 year olds were unemployed, and none were on training schemes like YTS – these did not then exist. By 1979, 7 per cent were unemployed and a further 6 per cent were on training schemes which were largely set up for the unemployed. By 1983, the equivalent figures here were 13 per cent and 19 per cent. The effective unemployment rates for these three years were: 3 per cent, 13 per cent, and 32 per cent. If anything, this understates the collapse of youth opportunities for work, as part of the increase in staying on at school over that period was probably due to the unavailability of employment.

Government explanations of youth unemployment tended to focus on skills, or the lack of them, and attitudes, eg an alleged unwillingness to work. It is difficult to see how either skills or attitudes could have changed so dramatically as to have produced such a rise in unemployment. It is more likely that much of this increase is explained in changes in the demand for labour, not changes in the quality of the labour supply.

THE CONSEQUENCES OF UNEMPLOYMENT – REAL AND FEARED

Concern about unemployment at the two ends of the working-age spectrum takes on different forms.

Youth

For the young unemployed, there have been concerns over:

- the alleged absence of relevant skills and appropriate values
- the growth of a so-called dependency culture
- long -term social exclusion
- an increase in youth crime, possibly drug related
- young parenting, with or without a partner/spouse.

Some of these tap into the recurring moral panic about youth (Pearson, 1983) and explain why governments have perhaps seen youth unemployment as a bigger problem than unemployment among other age groups. It is certainly the case that government spending on reducing unemployment has focussed much more on this age group than it has on the older unemployed: almost 10 times as much has been spent on them as on the latter (*The Guardian*, 5 January 1998).

Youth unemployment – a gendered experience?

It is not surprising that the experience and consequences of youth unemployment are different for young women than for young men. This has been shown in studies of the transition from education to the labour market. Gender differences have sometimes polarised around two themes:

1 Young women as single mothers, often depicted in stereotypical and stigmatising ways.
2 Young men as absent fathers and criminal offenders.

The older unemployed

For the older unemployed, there have been different concerns. One issue explored more fully in the section on old age itself (see p. 78), is that of unplanned, unwanted premature exit from the labour market. This disguised unemployment, and unemployment among men of middle age and above is associated with a range of problems and concerns:

- the risk of poverty, including, or perhaps especially, in old age
- poor health, both physical and mental
- suicide
- marital breakdown.

The significance of these risks has to be considered against the fact that a higher proportion of older unemployed people are long-term unemployed (ie over a year). In the summer of 1996, 58 per cent of the unemployed in the 55–65 age group had been unemployed for over a year, compared to 21 per cent of the 16–24 group and 41 per cent of the 25–34 group (Office of National Statistics, cited in Convery, 1997).

DISABILITY AND UNEMPLOYMENT

Disability is a physical and social concept. It is about limitations on full and equal participation in the life of the community created by barriers of a physical and social kind (Disabled People's International definition, 1981, cited in NSS, 1995). It is also a relative concept, in that there are *degrees* of disability. Using 'a relatively low threshold of disability', one survey estimated that there were 6.2 million people in Britain with a disability (Office of Population Censuses and Surveys, 1988, again cited in NSS, 1995). Of course, not all of these will be of working age, or, if so, in the labour market; some will have too high a level of disability for this.

Having said this, there is much evidence to suggest that people with disabilities who are in the labour market face considerable problems of prejudice, discrimination and access, all of which are social in origin. Problems like these – and other issues of disability – have been invisible in sociology for too long (Davies, 1994). Research by Barnes for the British Council of Organisations of Disabled People, published in 1991, showed evidence of discrimination in the labour market. Job applicants with a disability were six times more likely to be turned down than others; their unemployment rate was three times as high (cited in Davies, 1994). Other research states that, even where disabled and non-disabled people have identical qualifications and skills, the latter are well over twice as likely to get the job (cited in Spybey, 1997). More recent research showed that deaf people face greater difficulties in getting a job than people with a criminal record or a history of drug abuse (Royal National Institute for Deaf People, 1997, cited in *The Guardian*, 2 December 1997). It has to be said that this latter research was based on interviews with 100 'opinion leaders', and the findings reflect their views on the level of discrimination faced, rather than actual evidence of it.

The 1996 Act and the planned Disability Commission referred to on p 29 should reduce some of this discrimination.

See Chapter 6 on welfare for a short case study on disability and unemployment statistics (pages 126–128).

GENDER AND UNEMPLOYMENT

This section will be left deliberately short because the statistics on unemployment for men and women are hard to disentangle because of the problem of the numbers who have left the labour market or who are, for other reasons, economically inactive. In 1996, the percentage of working-age women who were economically inactive was twice as high as that for men – 28.4 per cent as opposed to 14.9 per cent (Office of National Statistics, in Convery). Trends in labour-market participation are, however, narrowing this gender gap. On the one hand, women's participation has been rising since 1979. On the other hand, the number of men of working age who have *left the labour market altogether* has been increasing, especially but not exclusively among the over-50s. This number was 800,000 in 1979 and 2.3 million in 1998 (Gregg, 1998).

As regards unemployment itself, it depends on which measure is used. **Convery** cites autumn-1966 data from the two different measures used, the official count and the Labour Force Survey – see Table 8.

Table 8: *Two measures of gender and unemployment ('000s)*		
	LFS	CLAIMAINTS
Men	1,415	1,434
Women	811	469

SOURCE: CONVERY, 1997.

Activity
Try to find out why the gender gap in unemployment is smaller on the first measure than it is on the second.

SUMMARY

- There are various ways of measuring the distribution of income, mainly depending on the extent to which taxes and benefits are taken into account.
- The postwar tax and benefit changes seemed to produce a somewhat more equal distribution of income in Britain, at least until the late 1970s.
- It is important to link income distribution to key social stratification variables like class, gender, ethnicity, age and disability. In doing this, it is important to consider the specific problems of operationalising some of these concepts, such as the importance of disaggregation when considering ethnicity.
- A central element in the exploration of income distribution, at least original income, is the relationship of the individual or the household to the labour market.
- There have been major changes in employment and unemployment patterns in the last few decades, including the decline of the full-time, permanent job and the increasing gap between work-rich and workless households. These changes have had a significant influence on the distribution of income.

EAST YORKSHIRE COLLEGE
ST.MARY'S WALK
BRIDLINGTON
NORTH HUMBERSIDE
YO16 5JW

Group work

People are notoriously unwilling to disclose how much money they earn. One way in which incomes from various forms of employment can be discovered is through job advertisements. Sources for these are:

1 local and national newspapers (choose a wide range to get a spread of job types)
2 the Job Centre
3 other media or display sources (eg agency windows).

Tasks:

1 Chart the advertised earnings of the jobs concerned in rank order and estimate the approximate degree of inequality from top to bottom.
2 Comment on this pattern in terms of the related characteristics of the jobs (type of work: part-time/full-time; manual/non-manual; type of industry; private or public sector and so on) and their likely incumbents (according to age, gender, qualifications, experience etc).

Research project

Income inequality may be seen as more or less legitimate. One theory (ie functionalism) suggests that inequalities in income reflect a widespread consensus on the functional importance of occupations.

Design a piece of research to test this idea. You may wish to focus on the views of a particular social group or on a wider sample of the population. Whichever approach you take, make sure that you consider the issue of generalisation in relation to sample type.

Practice questions

1 Evaluate sociological explanations of gender inequalities in incomes from employment.
2 Critically assess the view that income inequalities between ethnic groups in Britain cannot be solely explained by racial or ethnic discrimination.
3 'Statistics of employment, and especially of unemployment, do not measure the same phenomena that they did in the 1950s and 1960s.' Explain and discuss.

3

WEALTH, PROPERTY AND HOUSING

Introduction

INCOME PROVIDES ONE measure of inequality in society and perhaps the need for social welfare. A knowledge of the distribution of wealth and property gives another insight into the way privilege and deprivation are patterned according to class, age, gender and ethnicity. The study of wealth is also a central theme in the sociology of power and the culture of the wealthy is often a key element in the sociology of status patterns in society, though these issues belong more directly within the sociology of politics or of social stratification. Here the main focus is on the pattern of inequality itself and the way one type of property – housing – is linked to the need for social deprivation and welfare need.

DEFINING WEALTH

THE ASSETS THAT people possess take different forms. A common and important distinction is between marketable and non-marketable wealth. The former can be converted directly into money and then spent, if the owner so wishes. Obvious examples include bank deposits, stocks and shares, land, houses and other valuables. Included in many definitions is the wealth tied up in pension funds, both state and occupational. This wealth is real and a considerable asset, even where the owner cannot get at it to spend when they wish. Chapter 4 looks in detail at the pensions issue.

At the end of this chapter, there is a case study on housing. It looks at the pattern of ownership and how this has changed over time. In the long run, the values of houses, stocks and shares have generally risen, but there are important exceptions to this general trend. This is illustrated by the coining of a new phrase in the late 1980s. What happened to some people was as follows. After a

Table 9: *Issues, concepts and theories, and authors in sources in this chapter*		
KEY ISSUES	KEY CONCEPTS AND THEORIES	KEY AUTHORS AND SOURCES
The measurement of wealth, including its distribution/redistribution. Types and sources of wealth	Marketable and non-marketable wealth. 'Old money' and 'new money'; inheritance and entrepreneurialism. The 'super rich'	*Social Trends* Titmuss Adonis and Pollard Scott
The distribution of wealth, trends, patterns, associations (class, gender, ethnicity and age)	Regressive and progressive taxation	*Social Trends*
Housing tends and patterns	Housing tenure Polarisation and residualism Ideology	Murie Saunders Curtice
Homelessness: measures and patterns	Conflicting definitions of homelessness and housing adequacy	Official statistics; *Social Trends* Shelter and other campaign groups
Homelessness: explanations and consequences	Structural and cultural theories Social Exclusion	British Social Attitudes Surveys

mortgage had been taken out to buy a house at a particular price, the value of the house went down so that it became worth less than the amount the people in question had borrowed to pay for it. The loan was then bigger than the value of the house – hence *negative equity*. Where people had wealth tied up in property, as distinct from their own personal home, their wealth often fell also. It has been estimated that between 1989 and 1996, the average personal holding of wealth in Britain fell by over £6,000, mainly because of the slump in the property market.

Table 10 shows the pattern and trend in the distribution of measurable wealth between 1976 and 1993.

Table 10: *Measuring Wealth 1: marketable wealth*					
% OF MARKETABLE WEALTH OWNED BY:	1976	1981	1986	1991	1993
Most wealthy 1%	21	18	18	17	17
Most wealthy 5%	38	36	36	35	36
Most wealthy 10%	50	50	50	47	48
Most wealthy 25%	71	73	73	71	72
Most wealthy 50%	92	92	90	92	92

SOURCE: INLAND REVENUE, IN *SOCIAL TRENDS*, 26, 1996.

The figures are cumulative. Consider the following illustration to explain what this means:

- In 1976, the top 1 per cent owned 21 per cent of all personally held marketable wealth.
- The top 5 per cent owned 38 per cent.
- Therefore, the 4 per cent of the population who are in the wealthiest 5 per cent but who are not the top 1 per cent must have 17 per cent of all personal wealth between them (ie 38 minus 21).

What is interesting about this example is that it shows the gap between what might be called the very wealthy and the extremely wealthy: the richest 1 per cent of the population owned more than the next richest 4 per cent combined.

Study point
1   Was the 1976 pattern of the top 1 per cent owning more than the next richest 4 per cent in the top 5 per cent still the case in 1993?   2   What has happened generally to the pattern of ownership over the period shown in Table 10?

Figures on the cash and other directly liquid assets that people hold give a less abstract impression of the inequality of wealth in Britain than Tables 10 and 11. A survey by the Institute of Fiscal Studies 1991/92 showed the following:

- The poorest 10 per cent of households had no savings at all.
- Those in the next poorest decile had just £5.
- Half of all the households had less than £450.
- The average holding was £3,000.
- Those in the top decile had around £15,000; this, remember, is liquid or cash assets and is nearly 10 years ago.

SOURCE: *THE GUARDIAN*, 29 SEPTEMBER 1994.

THE DISTRIBUTION OF WEALTH — SOME RECENT INFLUENCES

One long-term change of significance in the form of wealth ownership has been the increase in house ownership; this is explored later in the chapter (see pp 52–54). Another is the spread of share ownership to a much wider percentage of the population than ever before.

This spread has mainly been the consequence of two developments that came in with the policies and ethos of Mrs. Thatcher's 1980s period in office. The first was the privatisation of many previously state-owned industries. The second was the so-called *de-mutualisation* of many building societies and friendly societies.

PRIVATISATION

Privatisation involves the government's selling of shares in state-owned industries so that these cease to be owned, through the government, by the *general* public and come to be privately owned by *particular members* of the public. This policy was a direct consequence of the Conservative General Election victory in 1979. This victory brought about a massive shift in social and economic affairs. Members of the public and employees in these industries were now encouraged to buy shares in these companies. This encouragement came in the form of huge media advertising campaigns and, more significantly here, considerable reductions in the prices of these shares to well below their market value.

DE-MUTUALISATION

The background to this is to be found in the ownership pattern of building societies and similar mutual-benefit institutions. Mostly set up in the nineteenth century by workers as a form of self-help and self-improvement, these institutions were owned by their members, the people who had accounts with them. They were run for the benefit of these member account holders, not for the private profit of a separate set of shareholders. In the 1980s, and subsequently, some of these institutions have become private companies, just like any other company run for profit. The existing members/account holders were issued with free shares in these new private companies, but from then on, new account holders would be just like customers of any other financial institution. These free shares, called 'windfalls' were worth hundreds, sometimes thousands of pounds, such as in the case when the Halifax Building Society de-mutualised.

Whilst there may have been a small increase in the numbers of the population buying shares on the British Stock Exchange, these two combined developments transformed the pattern of share ownership in a huge way. National Opinion Polls (NOP) and a private-share sponsorship organisation called Proshare gave the following outline of the numbers of private shareholders in Britain:

- 1979: estimated around 2 million.
- The end of the 1980s: 10 million, mainly the product of the privatisation programme. (This number fell a little in the early 1990s as some of the newer shareholders sold their privatisation shares for cash.)

- The mid 1990s: 15 million plus (mainly reflecting the impact of de-mutualisations).

SOURCE: THE OBSERVER BUSINESS SECTION, 22 JUNE 1997.

The significance of this widening of share ownership should not be underestimated, but neither should it be over estimated. The article just referred to pointed out that 80 per cent of shareholders own less than £5,000 worth of shares. Some of the holdings will be of just a few hundred pounds in value.

THE SUPER CLASS

The rise in the number of extremely large salaries being paid to directors both following privatisations and, more generally, in the law and the city, has led to the emergence of what has been called a 'Super Class' (Adonis and Pollard, 1998). These high salaries are associated with lifestyles to match the incomes 'earned': expensive holidays, private health and education; second homes in the country or abroad; servants, cleaners, nannies and so on. The wealth of this class is sometimes more concentrated because of patterns of intermarriage within the class, a reflection of the fact that women sometimes do reach the highest occupational echelons of today.

SOURCE: INLAND REVENUE, IN SOCIAL TRENDS, 26, 1996.

Table 11: *Measuring Wealth 2: marketable wealth plus pension rights*					
% OF MARKETABLE WEALTH PLUS OCCUPATIONAL AND STATE PENSION RIGHTS, OWNED BY:	1976	1981	1986	1991	1993
Most wealthy 1%	13	11	10	10	10
Most wealthy 5%	26	24	24	23	23
Most wealthy 10%	36	34	35	33	33
Most wealthy 25%	57	56	58	57	56
Most wealthy 50%	80	79	82	83	82

The pattern of wealth ownership shown in Table 11 is more equal than that based on marketable wealth only. This is not really surprising. State pensions have been a universal National Insurance benefit for most of the formerly employed population since 1946. A large and growing number of the employed population are now in occupational pension schemes as well.

POINTS OF EVALUATION – THE PROBLEM OF MEASURING
WEALTH RELIABLY

It is worth noting that measuring the value of pension rights is not easy, but nor is measuring the value of distribution of wealth itself. There are various reasons for this difficulty:

- Owners, for tax or other reasons, may conceal the true extent of their wealth. Some of the various strategies of concealment were discussed in a very influential text more than 40 years ago (Titmuss, 1958). For example, there may be family trusts which mask the extent to which wealth is concentrated in a few hands. Wealth may also be kept in holdings or banks overseas.
- The value of assets may genuinely be hard to assess accurately, such as with works of art or antiques. Alternatively, their value may change rapidly, usually upwards but sometimes downwards, such as with the value of property in the early 1990s. Many people found that the value of their only real form of wealth was worth less than the mortgage on it. Although the numbers with this negative equity fell over the 1990s, it still affected 500,000 households in 1996 (source: Woolwich Building Society, *The Guardian*, 8 October 1996).
- The main method used to calculate the ownership of wealth is through the estimated value of estates of people dying in a given year. In 1993, there was a technical change in the way these estates were calculated, making comparisons before and after that date not altogether reliable. Another problem is that many of the wealthy dispose of some of their wealth to their family members in the form of gifts so as to avoid tax on these estates. On Budget Day 1999, it was reported that the government was tightening up rules on the declaration of gifts made within seven years of the donor's death. This is the period in which inheritance tax still becomes liable on transfers of money or property. The budget did, however, increase the level at which this tax starts, to £231,000.
- In calculating the value of pension rights, there are a number of particular, but important, problems. Just one will be sufficient to illustrate the level of difficulty involved. Even if the calculation only looks at the basic state pension, which is the same each week for everyone, major problems emerge when considering factors like life expectancy. The value of these pension rights for those with longer life expectancy, such as the middle class, is greater than it is for the poor. Far more of the latter will die before they qualify for the pension rights to which they have contributed.

🔄

Study point

1   Describe the differences in the distribution of wealth in 1993 using the different measures in Tables 10 and 11.
2   How has the distribution of marketable wealth changed over the period shown in Table 10?
3   What percentages of marketable wealth have been owned by the poorest half of the population over the years shown in Table 10?
4   What percentages of marketable wealth, plus occupational and state pension rights, have been owned by the poorest half of the population over the years shown in Table 11?

NB: These last two questions are merely to direct attention to the statistics concerned if previous answers have not considered them.

WHO ARE THE RICH?

This section goes beyond the abstract and sociologically anonymous account of the distribution of wealth. It treads the familiar sociological path of relating these structural issues to the locational or positional questions of how this pattern of wealth connects to class, gender and ethnicity.

CLASS AND WEALTH

At one level, there is an element of the obvious here. If people are wealthy, there is a case for saying that they are 'upper class', or some other such term for that group of the population who are rich. There is much merit in this argument. However, what it does not address are two sets of questions of crucial significance to the sociological study of the rich. These are:

1   Did the wealthy start off life as rich? Is their money inherited, or was it acquired in their own lifetimes (ie self-made)? This is linked to the concepts of 'old money' and 'new money'.
2   What is the source of the wealth of the rich? Is it land, finance, business, entertainment – or something else?

Old Money and New Money

In Britain, being wealthy has traditionally been associated with inheritance, and to some extent with land ownership and titles. Part of the history of Britain since the Industrial Revolution has been the charting of the decline in the wealth, power and, perhaps, status of that land-owning class called the aristocracy. Whilst 'the landed estate and lifestyle' still carry significance, landowners per se are a less important category in that class now than they used to be (Scott, 1982).

Nonetheless, in 1976 it was still possible to claim that, 'The old money still absorbs the new, and still normally at one generation removed' (Giddens, 1976).

For a detailed breakdown of the richest in Britain, The *Sunday Times* list of the richest 1,000 families or individuals in Britain is an excellent source. In 1998, the list contained the following details:

- 693 are self-made millionaires.
- 307, about 30 per cent of the total, inherited their wealth. This is a declining percentage. In 1988, 57 per cent of the richest 200 had inherited their wealth.
- 145 had titles, though this does not mean that they were hereditary titles. The Queen is in there, of course, but so is life peer Lord Lloyd-Webber.
- As regards sources of wealth, with inherited wealth categorised according to its original source, only 69 were categorised as landowners, with 145 in industry, 84 in finance, banking, etc and 58 in music and entertainment. Just 2 were lottery winners, and only 3 were practising sportsmen (Nigel Mansell, Lennox Lewis, Nick Faldo).
- 75 went to Eton and 14 to Harrow. Some others went to other leading public schools, whilst the educational background of some is not known. 104 went to either Oxford or Cambridge, but only 3 to Newcastle University!
- 492 either live, or have their interests, in the South-east; the figure for Wales is 8.

Other evidence supports this idea of wealth concentration in the south-east, especially linked to the city (Adonis and Pollard, 1998).

What is sociologically significant about many of the people on this list is the way that they illustrate how much money can be accrued in a lifetime, or only part of one, without coming from wealthy backgrounds. Examples could be selected from the rich of the fashion business or the computer industry. Higher rates of social mobility than in the past, however, do not necessarily reduce the degree of inequality between the rich and the poor. Indeed, it may be easier for a social system to be legitimised if it allows for this millionaire mobility.

GENDER AND WEALTH

The *Sunday Times* list contains 979 men and 64 women. (This total is slightly higher than 1,000 because the list contains people entered as couples or members of the same wealthy family.) The list does not say how many of the women inherited their wealth from fathers or husbands. Some are famous in their own right, but compare their gender positions with their overall positions:

- Anita Roddick: 14th equal for women, joint 264th with her husband in the overall list;
- Jackie Collins: 44th equal for women, 769th equal in the overall list;
- Annie Lennox: 44th equal for women, 769th equal in the overall list;
- Delia Smith: 49th equal for women, 837th equal in the overall list;
- There is also the Queen, 6th for women, 94th equal in the overall list.

NB: Until 1994, the royal art collection was counted as part of the Queen's personal wealth. If this were still included, she would be worth between £5 and £10 billion and be the richest person in Britain and the richest woman in the world.

ETHNICITY AND WEALTH

Forty-three Asians are listed in the 1998 *Sunday Times* Rich List. This is not that much different from their percentage in the population as a whole. However, given their relatively recent arrival in Britain and their lack of connections here, a lower percentage in the top 1,000 might have been expected. Whilst many of the rich Asians are totally self-made wealthy, not all are. For example, Lakshmi Mittal is listed as the third richest person in Britain, with assets of £2 billion. His fortune is testimony to hard work, but his father was an Indian steel magnate. Martin Jacques has suggested that the moral and social values of some of the Asian settlers in this country are highly conducive to material success here. Certainly, they have been more successful in these terms than Afro-Caribbeans, with only one person in the Rich List. It may be that things here are due to change however. A study for Barclays Bank by Critical Research showed a new, thriving and optimistic black business sector, with many new businesses being set up in the previous three years (*The Journal*, a weekly independent black newspaper, 22 April 1997).

THE SELF-MADE WEALTH OF MANY ASIAN PEOPLE IN BRITAIN IS OFTEN SEEN AS TESTIMONY TO HARD WORK AND VALUES CONDUCIVE TO MATERIAL SUCCESS.

AGE AND WEALTH

One stereotypical image of the wealthy is of elderly aristocrats or businessmen, people who have inherited meony or accumulated it over their lifetimes. This image, however, does not always correspond to reality, as recent data on the wealthy under-30s show (*The Observer*, 11 April 1999). There is an interesting gender dimension to this. All the top 10 wealthiest young entrepreneurs are male, but only four of the top 10 wealthiest entertainers are – the Spice Girls (plus former member, Geri Halliwell) fill four of the top six places here. Of the top 10 wealthiest entrepreneurs, 8 made their money in telecoms and computers and the other two in the film industry. None *yet* had the scale of wealth that some young aristocrats are due to inherit.

HOUSING — A CASE STUDY IN PROPERTY FOR THE PEOPLE

Introduction

There are many, often interlinked, aspects to the understanding of housing from a wealth and welfare perspective. This account will consider them under two main headings:

1 patterns and trends in housing tenure
2 homes and homelessness.

There is also a brief discussion on why housing is, or ought to be, a central issue in the sociological understanding of modern British society.

Table 12: *Issues, concepts and theories, and authors and sources in this chapter*		
KEY ISSUES	KEY CONCEPTS	KEY AUTHORS AND SOURCES
Housing trends and patterns	Housing tenure Polarisation and residualism Ideology	Murie Saunders Curtice
Homelessness: measures and patterns	Conflicting definitions of homelessness and housing adequacy Social exclusion	Official statistics Shelter and other campaign groups British Social attidues surveys

THE INVISIBILITY OF HOUSING IN A LEVEL SOCIOLOGY

Housing rarely enters the 'A' level sociology syllabus in its own right, but its significance is testified to by the number of other areas where it appears as a significant social variable. For example, the material circumstances of the home are often cited as important in explaining class differences in health (Black) and education (Halsey). Housing tenure in the form of growing working class house purchase has been referred to in two controversial accounts of the changing nature of the working class, especially regarding its voting patterns. These are the 1950s embourgeoisement thesis (Zweig) and its 1980s reworking as a partial explanation of the Conservatives during that decade. (Crewe). Tenure type has also been explored over several decades in relation to crime rates (Morris, 1957; Bottoms and Baldwin, 1976).

From the perspective of this book, the relevance of housing could hardly be overstated. Few other issues combine a direct focus on *both* wealth and welfare as much as housing. Housing is a basic welfare need, as well as being the major source of most people's personal wealth. Generally, the type, quality and location of a person's house are also good indicators of their income. Housing is also an excellent way to illustrate the competing models of meeting welfare needs: collective provision versus individual marked-based solutions.

PATTERNS AND TRENDS IN HOUSING TENURE

Tenure
Very simply, tenure refers to the distinction between buying a house (or flat etc) and renting one, as well as to the categories of rental. The main rental categories are private and public (or social). The former is for profit whereas the latter was originally set up as a form of welfare to meet housing needs not met through the market. Most social housing is public or council, but in recent decades, housing associations with a charitable basis have become more significant in the social housing sector.

Changes in tenure patterns from 1900 to 1945
The twentieth century has seen a dramatic shift in tenure patterns. This shift, some of the explanations for it, and some of its consequences, will now be outlined.

The origins of local authority housing are to be found in the latter years of the nineteenth century when acts of Parliament empowered councils to build and subsidise housing for the working classes. This empowerment, coming as a result of public health worries, was for slum clearance rather than for the meeting of general housing needs.

It was not until 1919, after the First World War, that council housing to meet *general* housing needs was developed on a large scale. For the first time, there were the beginnings of a significant alternative to the market as a means of meeting housing needs. Unlike in health, education and social security, however, this social or collective alternative was never destined to be the dominant mode of meeting people's needs.

It has been noted that the main beneficiaries of this post First World War expansion of council housing were the skilled working class, or even the lower middle class, not unskilled labourers (Darke and Darke, 1979; Marwick). Interestingly, it was in this period also that some members of the skilled working class began to buy their own homes. This fragmentation of the working class through housing ownership tenure can be seen as a forerunner of the 1980s and 1990s debate over 'consumption cleavages' in the working class.

The change in tenure patterns over the period mentioned are illustrated in Table 13.

Table 13: *Housing tenure between the wars (%)*				
YEAR	HOME OWNER	PUBLIC RENTED	PRIVATE RENTED	OTHER
1914	10	1	80	9
1938	25	10	56	9

SOURCE: ADAPTED FROM FORREST ET AL, 1990.

Changes in tenure patterns from 1945 onwards

After the Second World War period, the above trends continued, and the ideology of house ownership became increasingly powerful. This can be seen in two ways. First, the desirability of house ownership took root in the middle class and, increasingly, in many sections of the working class. Second, apart from a brief period immediately after the war, the main political parties took it for granted that the house-purchase market would be the main way that people's housing needs would be met. In the language of social welfare provision, public housing was seen in residualist, rather than collectivist, terms. However, it was only with Mrs Thatcher's Conservative General Election victory in 1979 that outright hostility to local authority housing emerged at governmental level.

- By 1979, house ownership was already the majority pattern, with 55.3 per cent of all dwellings in this category. Its growth was boosted by the ideology just discussed, by full employment, job security and the increase in real incomes during the postwar economic boom. House ownership also had tax inducements and subsidies, including exemption from capital gains tax, and more significantly perhaps, a tax allowance could be set against the interest payable on the mortgage loan. In 1990, someone with a £60,000 mortgage would have gained over £90 per month in this tax subsidy (Halifax, in *The Guardian*, 10 March 1999). As state subsidies to the public rented sector were gradually abolished, it became increasingly hard to justify this tax allowance. Its value was reduced, and finally it was abolished in 1999.

- In 1979 also, council housing was at a plateau of over 31 per cent of all dwellings. This had risen only very slowly over the previous 20 years but was then set to decline significantly for the first time since local authority housing started. A simple political slogan points to the main explanation of this decline: 'the right to buy'. This refers to the Conservative Government's policy of forcing councils to sell their houses and flats to sitting tenants if they wished to buy. These sales often took place at prices well below the market value of the houses themselves, thereby subsidising the transfer of publicly owned assets to private hands. By 1997, one third of council tenants had bought their homes – some 2.2 million dwellings. Councils were forbidden to use the capital from these sales to build new homes (*The Guardian*, 5 January 1999).

- Figures from *Social Trends 26*, 1996, neatly encapsulate the scale of the change over the 1980s. 'One in seventy new homes in the United Kingdom were built by local authorities and new towns in 1994 compared to nearly one in two in 1976. By the mid 1990s, house ownership was pushing up towards the 70 per cent mark' (Woolwich Building Society, quoted in the *Guardian Education Supplement*, 8 October 1996). The expansion in home ownership seems to have slowed considerably, however, as many young people do not have sufficient incomes to afford deposits or mortgages. This view was put forward by the former chief housing economist at the Department of the Environment. He suggested that there would be little growth in the proportion of householders in owner occupation over the next 16 years (A. Holmans, quoted in *The Guardian*, 19 October 1995).

Theory and Tenure

Two theoretical considerations need to be explored before leaving the question of housing tenure. The first concerns the degree to which differences in housing tenure are associated with a polarisation in the housing market. The second concerns the ideology of house ownership that became associated with the Conservative Party in the 1980s.

Polarisation and Residualism

Residualism and social background.
It has already been noted that local authority housing was seen as a residualist rather than collectivist solution to meeting housing needs. As a consequence, there was bound to be some polarisation between council and private housing. The issue here is the degree to which this has become an *extreme* polarisation.

Alan Murie (1983) noted that this polarisation was partly brought about by the long-term switch of better-off private tenants to house purchase and of the less well off to the council rented sector. The outcome of these two trends was that

Supplementary Benefit claimants came to be more disproportionately represented within the council rented sector than was previously the case.

It has been said that the 'right to buy' scheme significantly increased the 'residualist' nature of public housing in two distinct ways (Forrest and Murie). One concerns the nature of the public housing stock; the other concerns the social composition of those leaving or remaining in this rented sector.

The residualist argument is that 'right to buy' purchasing was predominantly of the more desirable public housing stock, ie houses, especially those with gardens, rather than flats, particularly high-rise inner city flats. It also argues that the purchasing tenants were generally better off than the tenants who remained in council housing. This argument was explored in the 8th British Social Attitudes Report (Curtice, 1991).

Council tenants were more likely to be drawn from older age groups than were owner-occupiers, and were more likely to be working class, though interestingly the working class were more likely to be owner-occupiers than council tenants. Income patterns were also explored. It was found that 60 per cent of council tenants lived in households in the bottom income quartile.

However, the most significant variable differentiating council tenants and owner-occupiers was not class as such, but employment status. Council tenants were much more likely to be unemployed, retired or dependent on state benefit for some other reason. A question in the BSA survey asked the respondents if they, or anyone else in their household, had been in receipt of state benefit during the last five years. The answer brought the contrast, shown in Table 14, between council tenants and owner-occupiers.

Table 14: *Benefit and household status (%)*			
TYPE OF BENEFIT	OWNER-OCCUPIERS	COUNCIL TENANTS	ALL IN THE SURVEY
Unemployment Benefit	13	22	16
One-parent Benefit	2	11	4
Family Credit	1	12	3
Income Support	6	26	12
Housing Benefit	6	43	15

SOURCE: CURTICE, 1991.

Curtice goes on to look at other patterns and trends in housing tenure and social composition, and uses them to justify the residualist argument. The proportion of council tenants on social security and in the lowest income quartile is rising. In 1990, 38 per cent of owner-occupiers owned shares, compared with 8 per cent of council dwellers. Further support for the residualist argument comes from more recent research by the Centre for Housing Policy at York University. This shows the growing link between economic inactivity and the local authority or social housing sector. People with jobs tend to move out of this sector whilst those without jobs move into it: less than a quarter of heads of household in this sector now have employment (Burrows, 1997). The link between employment and the ability to obtain and pay a mortgage is an obvious factor here. This is also the case when employment type is considered. Part-time or self-employed workers are three times more likely to lose homes through mortgage arrears than people in permanent and full-time employment (Shelter, reported in *The Guardian*, 16 November 1998).

Whilst not directly relevant to the residualist argument itself, the data in Table 15 on the ethnic backgrounds of people in rented social housing is interesting to note here.

Table 15: *Ethnicity and rented social housing 1992–94*	
Ethnic group	% in rented social housing
Indian	7
Pakistani/Bangladeshi	24
Black	52
Other Ethnic Minority	33
White	24

Source: *Social Trends*, 26, 1996.

Study point

Refer to data on the demographic and socio-economic profile of these ethnic groups, either from other sections this book or from elsewhere. Does the data reinforce the residualist argument outlined here?

Residualism and housing type

As regards the type of housing within each tenure category, the BSA survey yielded the data shown in Table 16.

Table 16: *Housing types and tenure types*		
HOUSING TYPE	TENURE TYPE	
	COUNCIL RENTED	OWNER-OCCUPIED
Detached	< 1	28
Semi-detached	37	40
Terraced	34	26
Purpose-built flat	27	4

Study point

1 What does the evidence in Table 16 suggest about the link between housing tenure and housing type?
2 Does this evidence reinforce or challenge the residualist argument?

Study point

This study point involves evaluation, validity and the operationalisation of concepts. The accommodation types shown in Table 16 to are not simply different in architectural terms. They are being used as measures of something about housing quality, however approximately. The general assumption is that housing advantage/disadvantage can be plotted, or measured, along a continuum from detached to purpose-built flat, as in the table. There may be significant, if general, justification for this. However, good measures are not always perfect measures.

In order to assess the validity of this continuum as a measure of housing advantage/disadvantage, try to list *two different reasons* for *each* accommodation type that would either support or weaken its claim to validity. An example to start you off is that of purpose-built flats – these can include luxury penthouse accommodation for the very rich.

(NB: You may have referred to some of these accommodation types in the study point just before.)

Residualism, housing conditions and housing quality
There is growing evidence that the quality of the housing stock in the public sector has deteriorated relative to that in owner occupation. This is particularly true of the least popular housing estates which have become one of the priorities for the Social Exclusion Unit set up by the government after the 1997 election. One measure of the quality of housing as experienced by residents is the degree of overcrowding. Research indicates a close link between this and housing tenure. Thus, in 1999, it was reported that 25 per cent of households in social rented accommodation were overcrowded, compared to under 10 per cent for those on a mortgage and less than 4 per cent for those living in homes owned outright (*The Guardian*, 5 January 1999).

Footnote – polarisation in the owner-occupied sector
It should not be thought that polarisation by tenure type is the only social division based on housing. Indeed, there is evidence that the spread in house ownership has coincided with the creation of a gulf within this sector. This is between those owners of highly valued properties who can afford to repair and maintain them, and another group altogether worse off. In 1981, only 5 per cent of non-pensioner mortgage households were unemployed or economically inactive (Murie, 1997). By 1996, over 10 per cent of them were unemployed or economically inactive (Howarth et al. 1998). There are house owners and there are house owners!

2 The ideology of home ownership
The general popularity of home ownership seems undeniable, but there is a sociological dispute about what the basis of that popularity is. One view comes from New Right theorist **Peter Saunders**. He sees the popularity as coming from two related sources:

- First, there are the financial rewards that he sees as more or less inevitably stemming from house ownership.
- Second, he sees house ownership as meeting the needs that he believes people have for possessions and independence. These needs are said to stem from an intrinsic human need for autonomy. The desire for house ownership, therefore, is seen as natural and inevitable.

Points of evaluation of Saunders' argument
Forrest et al. argue against Saunders in the following way. The financial gains from house ownership are not guaranteed. They are partly contingent on such circumstances as state subsidies through tax exemptions and allowances. The gains have also become less certain as house ownership has increased, bringing into the sector people and housing whose incomes and market values, respectively, are much less assured.

The British Social Attitudes survey evidence
The BSA survey confirms the growing popularity of house purchase and indicates a higher level of housing satisfaction than in the council sector, even where housing type (detached etc) is accounted for. This gives some support to Saunders' view.

However, when the survey looked at *why* council tenants had a higher dissatisfaction rating with their housing, Saunders' concerns about lack of personal autonomy and the degree of landlord control were hardly mentioned. On another point also, Saunders' overall thesis was questioned. This is the alleged immutability of the desire for house ownership, regardless of social and economic changes or conditions. Curtice found that the downturn in the housing market in the late 1980s and early 1990s did lead to an increased scepticism about the benefits of house ownership. This may, of course, only be temporary.

Some comparative data of an international kind seems to question Saunders' view that the popularity of house ownership is based on some natural need for autonomy. A study of 12 nations shows Britain near the top of the house ownership league but with some countries having comparatively small owner-occupied sectors. The Netherlands had only 45 per cent and Switzerland was even lower at 28 per cent (Oswald, 1996, cited in *The Independent*, 25 April 1997).

HOMELESSNESS AND RELATED PROBLEMS

This section will look at the various methodologies used in measuring homelessness and at the main types of theory used in explaining it. It will also consider some of the consequences of homelessness.

1 Methodology and the measurement of homelessness
There are many ways to define homelessness. Different definitions produce different measures, and obviously, the narrower the definition, the lower the number of people who count as homeless.

The sleeping rough count and other 'common sense' measures
The sleeping-rough count may be said to be the 'common sense' measure, if common sense is defined in a rather harsh way. Another, more liberal 'common sense' definition might say that anyone without an adequate home is homeless; this is discussed in the third example of measurement approaches. The sleeping-rough count can be defined as an absolute measure in the way that some have attempted to define poverty (see pp. 92–93). However, those in hostels and so on are only there because they are homeless, and therefore, should really be included in any absolute definition of homelessness.

There are no regular, reliable figures kept for the homeless who sleep rough. Strong impressionistic evidence points to a dramatic rise in the 1980s; indeed, it barely existed throughout most of the later postwar years until that decade.

In 1998, the Government's Social Exclusion Unit estimated that there were 2,000 people sleeping rough in Britain, 400 of them in London. A 1989 Salvation Army partial survey of those sleeping rough in London counted over 750. Nearly all of these were white, and 88 per cent were male. A different gender and ethnic profile came from figures on young London homeless from the homeless charity Centrepoint in 1994. Its data included people using its six London hostels, and showed that 44 per cent of the group were from ethnic minorities and that an increasing number were young homeless women.

In addition to this number, the Salvation Army pointed to another 18,000 or so in hostels, 25,000 in bed and breakfast hotels and 30,000 in squats. This makes a total of about 75,000 homeless in London using this definition. Estimates by the London Resource Centre in 1986/87 suggested that 130,000 were homeless in the sense of being without their own accommodation but this included those staying with friends and relatives.

The official count
This count is important from a welfare perspective because it is only by being homeless on this definition that people can obtain housing assistance from a local authority. The background to the situation is this. Up until 1977, the official count of the homeless was the number of people housed by social welfare agencies. In 1977, for the first time ever, the Homeless Persons Act imposed on local councils an obligation to provide housing for the homeless. The discussion here is based on the general principles of this Act, although there were some policy changes brought in by another Act in 1985.

Certain groups were exempt from its provisions, most notably single people, unless they had children or were pregnant. Crucially, the Act required that people had to be unintentionally homeless before they could register. The question of intentionality has been interpreted quite differently by different local authorities, as an Audit Commission report in 1988 showed. This report illustrated that people who had left their homes to seek work were defined as intentionally homeless by 55 per cent of local authorities but accepted as unintentionally homeless by 29 per cent (*The Observer*, 6 November 1988). This variation indicates problems with the reliability of the official count.

Points of evaluation
Clearly, this official definition excluded some people who were 'really' homeless because the government did not feel that these groups should get state-provided accommodation. This shows that the government's definition cannot be taken as

a valid measure of homelessness. This is a similar situation to that of not counting as unemployed those people whom the government has disqualified from unemployment benefit. (See pp. 30–32.)

There are many reasons why sociologists are sceptical of official measures of social problems, such as homelessness. A general explanation of this is to be found in the 'debunking tendency' or 'art of mistrust' that is an essential element of the sociological approach to official accounts of society (Berger, 1963). Thus, in terms of government image, social-problem statistics might be seen as measures of government failure. Governments, therefore, have a vested interest in constructing or presenting these statistics in ways that do least harm to this image.

Another, more directly policy-related implication of the measurement of social problems concerns the cost of tackling them. Where governments are expected 'to do something about' social problems like homelessness, a high-number measure of the problem will produce a solution that is more expensive. This may mean that governments are drawn towards the narrower definition of the problem, especially governments that espouse a low-spending ideology of the state.

The increase in official homelessness
Official homelessness increased considerably throughout the 1980s. In 1970, the number of households accepted as homeless was under 8,000 (*The Observer*, 6 November 1988). Department of Environment figures showed homeless household numbers in England and Wales rising from under 60,000 in 1978 to 120,000 in 1988. These 120,000 households represented 370,000 people. (*The Guardian*, 29 December 1988). More recent homelessness figures can be found in *Social Trends*.

Activity

Locate a copy of *Social Trends* in a library.
1 The 1985 Housing Act which replaced the 1977 Act required councils to house people who were in one or other category of 'priority need'. What groups of the population do you think would come into this category? Check your answer against the data on this in *Social Trends*. Note the relative numbers in each category housed by local authorities.
2 Local authorities also keep data on the reasons why people that they find accommodation for have become homeless. What do you think are the main reasons why people find themselves homeless? Check your ideas against the data in *Social Trends*.

The adequacy count

The term 'adequacy' has been chosen so that the homelessness measure takes account of what might reasonably be expected of a home, so that it should take account of the *quality* of people's housing.

Given that what counts as adequate housing varies over time and between societies, this is a relative definition of homelessness. Like relative definitions of poverty, however, it is fraught with problems. These problems are not necessarily to do with the principle of defining homelessness in relation to certain standards of housing. Rather, they are more often to do with converting this idea into measurable, and hopefully agreed, standards. In short, they are to do with the operationalisation of the concept of homelessness defined in relative terms.

Although 99 per cent of all households now have the basic amenities of bath/shower and inside toilet (*Social Trends*, 1996), there are still major problems with the quality of housing stock. A Department of Environment survey of 25,000 dwellings carried out in 1991 found that 1.5 million were 'unfit for human habitation'. Some of these lacked an inside toilet, and two in five were in a serious state of disrepair (The English Household Conditions Survey for 1991).

Points of evaluation

A word of caution about the principle of this adequacy definition is necessary, however. Just as relative poverty cannot be simply equated with someone being less well off than the majority, so this definition of homelessness cannot be used to describe people whose houses are simply of lower quality than those of the majority. Nonetheless, it does highlight a real problem of defining and measuring homelessness. This is the problem of how to classify people who do have somewhere to live but whose accommodation is grossly unsatisfactory. At the very least, it shows that complete homelessness is not the only measure of serious housing deprivation.

Whilst on this issue of housing adequacy and deprivation, it is worth noting Murie's argument that definitions of housing deprivation take too little account of external factors. The availability of health and education facilities, as well as traffic and industrial pollution, could be included here. The real, or perceived, social problems of living on some housing estates might also be considered as forms of housing deprivation. These problems, such as litter, vandalism, drunks and so on, were looked at in the British Social Attitudes survey already referred to (Curtice, 1991).

2 *Theoretical perspectives on homelessness – structural or cultural problem?*

The wider, sociological significance of the structural/cultural debate is that it strongly resonates with conflicting explanations of poverty and of class differences in health and education. With some simplification, it is true to say that left wing theorists have tended towards structural explanations of homelessness (and poverty, etc.) and right wing theorists towards cultural explanations.

This section is intended to indicate some of the main issues in this debate rather than give a comprehensive account of all the possible causes of homelessness. In so doing it takes a case-study approach, focussing mainly on one particular group as an illustration of some general trends and arguments.

Study point

Before reading the next sections, write a list of possible explanations for homelessness, and suggest, for each, whether they are best seen as structural or as cultural factors. Indicate also, if you can, which of these explanations would be most likely to be adopted by a left wing perspective and which by a right wing one.

Homelessness and the young

The social construction of the "sham homeless"

It is in relation to homelessness among *young* people that cultural explanations of homelessness have been most frequently expressed, particularly in the popular press and some political circles. More particularly, it has sometimes been argued that young people sleeping rough, and sometimes begging, often fall into one of two categories. There are those whose situation is said to be self-inflicted and can be remedied by self-help, and there are those whose plight is said to be a sham and who are frauds pretending to have nowhere to live. In both categories, it is culture and lifestyle that are seen as problematic. Prime Minister John Major, for example, argued that, 'They are not on the streets because they have to be … . It is a strange way of life that some of them choose' (*The Guardian*, 25 April 1994).

Causes of homelessness among the young

In contrast to the arguments in the previous section considering research into youth homelessness over the past decade or so, a number of themes stand out quite distinctly: youth unemployment, benefit cuts, family breakdown and conflict, and inadequate social support for young people leaving care. In the late 1980s, changes to Housing Benefit regulations and levels in particular left many young people unable to obtain accommodation in bed and breakfast hotels, and many thus turned to sleeping rough. (The rise in youth unemployment and the abolition of unemployment benefit for 16/17 year olds in 1988 is covered in Chapter 2.)

The situation of young people leaving care was highlighted in a report for the Centrepoint housing charity in 1991. This report noted that just 0.6 per cent of the under-18 population was in local authority care but that 41 per cent of the young people using their hostel facilities had been in care. This reflects on the often extremely poor education received by those in care, their difficult or absent family circumstances, and the other employment, benefit and support-service issues just referred to (*The Guardian*, 15 July 1991).

At a wider level, there are clearly many problems with the supply of *affordable* accommodation to buy or rent. This is not primarily an issue of the total number of households, though changes in patterns of living mean that there has been a huge growth in the demand for dwellings. Rather, one of the main reasons for this supply problem has been the sale of council houses. This was reinforced by the government prohibiting councils from spending the £5.5 billion raised by these sales (1994 figures) on building homes to rent.

Homelessness and disability

Before leaving this section on homelessness, some research on how homelessness can affect other disadvantaged groups is worth considering. This is in line with this book's attempt to give a higher sociological profile to issues of stratification and inequality given insufficient coverage elsewhere.

A report for Shelter indicated that, between 1980 and 1986, homelessness among the disabled and mentally ill rose faster than it did for the general population (Morris, 1988 (see Table 17)).

Table 17: *Population group and homelessness increase*		
POPULATION GROUP	1980–86 % INCREASE IN HOMELESSNESS IN LONDON	1980–86 % INCREASE IN HOMELESSNESS IN ENGLAND
Physically handicapped	121	99
Mentally ill	146	92
General population	70	57

Study point

Describe the main findings in the table above. Avoid simply rewriting the data in a list of findings – be selective and analytical.

3 Some consequences of homelessness

Many of the consequences of homelessness are in the domain of health and a full account of these is beyond the remit of this book. Nonetheless, the significance of housing as a social policy issue cannot be assessed without a consideration of some of these consequences.

As some of the discussion of homelessness has focussed on young people, it is fitting here that some of the consequences of it be illustrated through an exploration of housing and children and young people.

The material for this section comes from the excellent report on the circumstances of Britain's children in relation to the commitments that the UK undertook when it signed the United Nations Convention on the Rights of the Child. Article 27 of this Convention concerns the right to a standard of living adequate for physical, mental, spiritual, moral and social development. The UK Agenda report notes that:

Access to adequate housing is a pre-requisite for the healthy development of a child. Without it, a child's right of access to education, health and health care, and social development are at risk ...

UK Agenda, 1994

The report then goes on to refer to evidence of the problems experienced by children in families living in bed and breakfast hotels for the homeless. These include: high levels of school absences, poor diets, high rates of accidents and infections, a lack of play space and long periods of effective confinement in hotel rooms. The families themselves will suffer high levels of stress and may be more at risk of marital breakdown or other indicators of conflict or difficulty.

Beyond these specific considerations are the general ones associated with the concept of social exclusion. Homeless people, or those who frequently move because of they have no permanent home, are less likely to be on the electoral register. They will also find it harder to keep registered with doctors and dentists, and will have children with disrupted educational careers.

European footnote

Some of the problems of measurement, and some of the possible explanations of homelessness, are placed in a wider perspective by a 1993 European report (1993 European Federation of National Organisations Working with the Homeless, or Feantsa, reported in *The Guardian*, 25 September 1993). The report estimates that there were 2.5 million homeless people in Europe during 1991/92, based on numbers using state or voluntary agencies for assisting the homeless. This was about 7.5 per cent of the population. It did not include people who did not seek assistance, maybe because they had stayed with friends. If they, along with other hidden homeless and those immediately at risk, were included, the report estimates that up to 5 million would be in this category. There were very large variations in the homelessness rates between member countries, with Britain and Germany near the top and Denmark and Portugal near the bottom. The contrast is stark: in Britain, 12.2 per cent were homeless, compared with less than 1 per cent in Denmark. Some of the variation could be due to different methods of reporting. In other words, the figures are not complete measures of the reality they are intending to depict; rather, they can be seen to some extent, as artefacts or social constructs.

What is interesting, but not surprising, is how those most at risk are those already vulnerable in social and economic terms. Thus, about 20 per cent of homeless were migrants from outside the European Community (now the European Union), 20 per cent were formerly in mental hospitals or prisons, and very high proportions came from people with low levels of education and training.

SUMMARY

- Privately owned wealth is concentrated in relatively few hands, despite the spread of home ownership and the growth in share ownership. Some relatively minor redistribution downwards did seem to take place in the first part of the postwar period. The sources from which wealth is derived are changing; inherited wealth remains important but has become less significant overall.
- House purchase has become by far the most common type of housing provision. This is most people's biggest ever purchase and only major source of wealth. Most other people have come to rely on rented social housing, which expanded in provision over the twentieth century until the end of the 1970s.
- Privately owned accommodation is generally different in type and quality from rented accommodation, especially that in the social rented sector. Generally, owners are advantaged, both socially and economically, compared to people living in the rented sector. There are also differences in the incomes, assets and quality of housing of those *within* the house-owning group.
- Some people's housing needs are so poorly met that they are homeless, and experience degrees of social exclusion. Homelessness, and other forms of unmet housing need, are often correlated with age, disability, ethnicity and, of course, class.

STUDY GUIDES

Group work

The section on housing tenure raises many questions about the ideology and apparent desirability of house ownership, as well as more general issues of housing satisfaction according to housing tenure and type.

Task: select one (or more) of these issues and construct a hypothesis around it (them), or set other specific research aims with such issues in mind. Design a piece of research to be carried out in your local area that would allow you to meet your research goal(s). For background to your research, you might find it useful to collect some data on such issues as house prices (estate agents' windows and the local paper would help here). See Saunders' or Curtice's work for assistance in formulating an hypothesis.

Coursework suggestions

Images of wealth: this project is particularly suitable for students who are also studying the media as part of their course. Others can obviously attempt it, but research on the media, whether using quantitative methods like content analysis or qualitative methods like semiology, can be more difficult than it seems.

The strategy would be to select particular media forms, such as a specific newspaper or set of newspapers, and then analyse the representation of the rich or wealthy over a period of time. Issues to consider could include: age/gender/ethnic profile and so on; money type: 'old' or 'new', and what source of the latter; lifestyle features; values implied (glamour/envy/role modelling/injustice/exploitation/etc).

Practice questions

1 What have been the main consequences of the spread of house ownership in contemporary Britain?
2 Give a sociological account of the changing wealth distribution pattern in postwar Britain.
3 Why are data on the distribution of wealth so difficult to rely upon?

NB: Question 3 is best seen as a mini-essay for 10 marks, rather than the traditional type worth 25 marks.

4

ELDERLY PEOPLE IN SOCIETY

Introduction

THIS CHAPTER EXPLORES the the inequalities in the material and welfare circumstances of elderly people according to their class, gender and ethnicity. Consideration is given to the different sources of income and welfare that people draw on in their old age: the state, the market, their families. In some senses, the chapter also acts as a case study, illustrating at a particular level many of the main, general issues of inequality and welfare.

A major aim of the chapter is to demonstrate that understanding society is impossible without understanding older people and their place within it.

OLD AGE AND INVISIBILITY

If you are reading this book as a fairly typical 'A' level student of 17 or 18, consider the fact that you might well spend more years in retirement than your whole life has lasted so far. This is especially so if you are female and therefore have a life expectancy of some five years more than your male class mates. Now consider the fact that some leading text books of sociology spend a whole chapter on one of the key life processes of childhood and youth, ie schooling. They also often devote significant space to the deviance and subcultures of youth.

Finally, consider the fact that the elderly hardly get a mention in many of these large tomes. They may crop up as a small section on the extended family or as an aspect of the coverage of poverty. They do feature more in health, and especially, in welfare chapters of books, but even here, not always very much. In any case, such coverage tends to reinforce the social-problem view of old age. As regards

Table 18: *Issues, concepts and authors and sources in this chapter*		
KEY ISSUES	KEY CONCEPTS	KEY AUTHORS AND SOURCES
Social definition of old age	Old age as a social construct; rites of passage; dependency; social problem perspective	Townsend Foucault
Inequalities and difference among the elderly: Class Gender Ethnicity	Proletarianisation and labour-market continuity theories Social exclusion Stereotyping Ethnic disaggregation	Demographic data from: GHS Arber Ginn and Arber
Income and wealth; the social division of welfare	The social division of welfare: state pensions and benefits; private pensions; tax allowances	Titmuss
Caring for the elderly: the alleged decline of the family; institutions – homes and hospitals; the decline of NHS provision	Community care Institutionalisation	Finch Anderson Goffman

chapters in mainstream areas of sociology, like those on work and leisure or social stratification, old age often barely gets a mention. This is despite the fact that many adults spend about a third of their lives in retirement.

INVISIBILITY AND STRATIFICATION THEORY

Arber (1989) notes that classical stratification theorists, such as Marx and Weber, ignored old age. The focus of stratification theory and research influenced by these writers has been the public domain of employment and the market. This has also accounted for the previous exclusion of women from many stratification studies and theories. Even when the elderly were the focus of research or theory, there was a tendency to see them in social-problem terms. There was also a tendency to define their situation in age-specific terms, part of an inclination to see the elderly as a homogenous group.

This book inevitably has some elements of a social-problem perspective on the elderly but it also seeks to take the debate much further.

⊜

Activity
1   Group Activity – Content Analysis Take the main general textbooks in your sociology room, or school/college library. Distribute them to individuals according to the number of books and students. Go through the list of contents and the index and count the number of references to old age, retirement or related words or ideas. 2   *Pairs* Draw up a list of the reasons of why you think the study of elderly people may not feature very much in sociology at A level.

There are three reasons why sociology needs to consider old age more fully than it does at present:

1   demographic factors
2   ageing as an important social process in its own right
3   ageing as a key feature in class, gender or ethnic experience.

DEMOGRAPHIC FACTORS

Demography is the study of population structure, size and change. It is more valuable in the understanding of society than most sociology textbooks give credit for, and is an essential tool for the understanding of old age in society.

There can hardly be anyone who is unaware that we live in an ageing society. We all know that people are living longer and longer. The idea of an ageing society is not just that people are living to an older age. It is not just about the growing number of people over retirement age either. Rather it is about the growing *proportion* of people over retirement age. This proportion is a product not just of their absolute numbers but also of the numbers below that age as well. A low birth rate, such as that found in modern Britain, means that the number of young, relative to the number of old, is declining and thus contributing to the ageing of society.

The simple facts are these. In 1901, over-65s made up just 5 per cent of the population. By 1994, the proportion of the population over 65 was, at 16 per cent, the highest it had ever been (sources: Ryder and Silver, 1972, and *Social Trends*, 1996). Table 19 shows projections for this elderly population, placed within the context of selected European countries.

A point to note

In concluding this section, it should be noted that the overwhelming majority of today's over-65s have left the labour market. Their circumstances cannot be understood in exactly the same ways as those of younger adults of working age. To ignore such a large, and in many ways distinct, group of the population is sociologically unjustifiable.

Table 19: *Proportions of over-65s in selected European countries, 1993, and projections for 2025*		
COUNTRY	1993 (%)	2025 (%)
Sweden	18.6	21.2
Italy	15.9	25.1
Britain	15.8	19.0
Germany	15.1	22.9
Greece	14.8	23.9
Romania	11.6	17.1
Poland	10.7	16.4
Turkey	4.4	9.2

SOURCE: ADAPTED FROM GIARCHI AND ABBOT, 1997.

2 AGEING AS A SOCIAL PROCESS IN ITS OWN RIGHT

Growing old is a chronological and biological fact. The body changes with age, and death is an eventuality that none of us can escape, but these simple truths tell us little of the social experience of old age. This experience of old age is a social one because it is society that defines what it is to be old and what meaning, expectations and status are attached to it. This is what is meant when sociologists say that old age, like age in general, is socially constructed. Three examples can be used to illustrate this idea of old age as socially constructed.

The definition of old age

In contemporary industrial societies, old age is often defined by reference to retirement. This is an economic status – or lack of it – and it bears no specific or necessary relation to biological changes in people. Retirement itself is a product of a wage-labour society, and more specifically of one where there is provision for income when employment has ceased, i.e. pensions.

The definition of old age based on retirement age, produced, in Britain at least, the odd situation of population statistics for the elderly having different sets of data for men and women. This is because the retirement age is currently 60 for women and 65 for men. The two ages are being brought into line at 65 for both sexes in 2010. This clearly illustrates one of the defining elements of a socially constructed phenomenon: that it is relative and therefore subject to variation over time.

One other aspect of the social construction through retirement in the modern era is the development of institutions (from workhouses to geriatric hospitals to nursing homes) and professionals (medical and welfare) that regulate the lives of older people. Whilst these processes and people are often seen in benign and positive terms, the work of the French philosopher and social theorist **Michel Foucault** points to more oppressive features of these power relations (Foucault, 1977). In these developments, the expert is the subject and the older person is the object. These ideas have some resonance with those of **Erving Goffman**, whose work on living in institutions was partly behind some of the criticisms of residential care in homes and hospitals for the elderly. These ideas are explored more fully later in the chapter.

The burden model of the elderly and the dependency ratio

Over the last few years, there has been a lot of negative discussion about the present, and especially future, costs of the growing elderly population. Much of this discussion can be criticised for its poor understanding, let alone for the values that seem implicit in its arguments. Criticising these arguments in terms of their poor understanding is directly a sociological task. Criticising the arguments in terms of their values is less so and more in line with a social-problem perspective on issues than a sociological one.

Sometimes, the language of the debate is quite apocalyptic, with references to a 'demographic time-bomb.' This imagery often reflects political ideology rather than sound understanding. Thus, in the 1980s, the Conservatives cut the future value of the State Earnings Related Pension Scheme (SERPS) on the basis that the growth of the elderly population meant that such pension provision could not be afforded. Their solution was that people should take out private pensions, but this obviously does nothing about the growth in the numbers of the elderly. Rather, what it does demonstrates their preference for market solutions over state solutions to social welfare problems.

There is one aspect of the 'demographic time-bomb' scenario that cannot be disputed, even though its interpretation can be. This is the fact that there will be a rise in the number of retirement pensioners in the twenty-first century, especially as the postwar baby boomers of 1946–48 come to retirement. However, the extent to which this justifies the 'scary vision' portrayed by some writers can be disputed. (Atkinson, *The Observer Business Section*). Kevin Gardiner, a financial economist, argues that:

---

the crude demographic arithmetic is misleading. The age profile of the population is only one of the many factors influencing the dependency burden.

One of the other factors is the *overall* extent of labour-market participation. On this wider measure, Britain's high rate of women's employment means that the alleged problem of an ageing population is not as great as it would otherwise be. Finally, on this issue, the views of the Director of the Institute of Fiscal Studies are worth noting. With direct reference to whether or not Britain can afford future welfare commitments, he says that, 'there is no economic law determining the right level of taxation or public spending.' (A. Dilnot, *The Observer*, 30 March 1997). To pretend otherwise is simply the exercise of ideology, covering up a political or ethical choice under the pretence that no choice is possible.

The experience of old age

One aspect of the experience of old age is how the old are treated by the rest of society. This is not just a question of people's personal qualities, such as kindness or respect for others. Clearly these can be important at the level of individual difference, but they cannot explain why the elderly in one society are treated quite differently from the elderly in another; this requires a sociological rather than an individualist account (C. Wright Mills, 1970).

In making such comparative analyses of the treatment of the elderly in different societies, sociologists often contrast the situation of the elderly in traditional societies with that of those in modern societies. At a very simple level, and at the risk of some overgeneralisation, this comparison suggests the following. In traditional societies, the skills and knowledge, and probably values also, acquired by the elderly as they grow older are those which are passed on to new generations. This means that their knowledge and such like still has currency, still has status – and so do they. On the other hand, modern societies tend to involve built-in social and technological change. Here, the knowledge, skills and values people acquire as they grow become less – or seen as less – relevant as time goes by. The status of the elderly is accordingly reduced. One feature of their reduced status in such societies is the degree to which their lives are partly structured around dependency (Townsend, 1981).

A post-modern view

Clearly, this traditional–modern comparison is an overgeneralisation, and some argue that it is becoming, or will become, less significant as Britain moves into a so-called post-modern era. The idea of post-modernism is a controversial one. It suggests that developments in technology, production, leisure and consumption are acting to undermine existing ideologies and belief systems. As part of this, ideas about old age become challenged, and older people become freer to adopt identities and lifestyles that are less constrained by the rigid ageism of earlier years. This optimism about the deconstruction and reconstruction of old age has to be tempered by an awareness of the continuing prejudice, discrimination and deprivation that many older people throughout Europe experience (Giarchi and Abbott, 1997).

3 AGEING AS A KEY FEATURE OF CLASS, GENDER AND ETHNIC EXPERIENCE

As the first section briefly indicated, the definition of old age through retirement is set differently for women and men. This is just one small example of the way in which the whole experience of ageing is different for the two genders/sexes. It is appropriate to use both terms here, gender and sex, as the differences in the ageing process for women and men are rooted partly in biological factors and partly in social and cultural factors. It is the latter that interest us most here, of course.

Activity
Work in pairs or small groups. Make a list of the ways in which old age may differ for men and women. For each factor identified, suggest a possible explanation and decide whether the difference is best understood as a result of biology or of society, or of both. Here is an idea to start off your list: retirement from work: what different impacts does this have on men and women?

The aim of the above activity is to demonstrate that it is impossible to understand gender differences in society if the focus stops at 60 or 65. The same applies to class and ethnicity. To assume otherwise is to treat the elderly as if knowledge of their age was all the knowledge needed to understand them – an extreme case of master status in operation (Becker, 1963). The class, gender and ethnicity differences amongst the elderly will be considered in some detail in the next section.

RESOURCES IN OLD AGE

If old age, however defined, is usually accompanied by departure from the labour market, then any understanding of the social and economic circumstances of old-aged people has to consider what assets they take with them into old age and what pension awaits them.

THE FIRST PENSIONS

The first old age pensions in Britain were introduced in 1908. They were selective, or means-tested, to focus only on the very poorest, and were paid for out of general taxation, ensuring some vertical redistribution of income in favour of the poor.

It was not until 1946 that a more or less comprehensive retirement pension scheme was introduced. This pension was based on National Insurance contributions and was available to all who had paid them. It was, therefore, a universal benefit, available as of right, not as a product of means testing. However, even in this national system, there were gaps, such as in the way women and people with disabilities were treated. The pension was set at a lower level than intended in the Beveridge Report, and straight away, many pensioners had to rely on additional state support in the form of means-tested National Assistance (now Income Support).

POSTWAR DEVELOPMENTS IN PENSION PROVISION

The declining value of the state basic pension

One of the main issues since then has been the changing value of the basic retirement pension. Governments decide what this level should be. The policy will depend on their political ideology, their perception of what can be afforded and their view of what is politically acceptable.

Activity

From 1948 to 1993, the real value of the single person's state pension more than doubled, from just over £20 per week to about £50 per week, measured at 1993 prices (John Hills, quoted in *The Guardian*, 14 March 1994). In August 1997, the single pension was worth £62.45 (at 1997 prices), £8.90 a day to cover everything.

Find out the current value of the state pension for single people and married couples.

On another measure of its value, the pension looks somewhat different. This looks at what the pension is worth as a percentage of average personal disposable income. This measure showed a somewhat fluctuating pattern over the period, with a small overall increase up to the early 1980s. What happened then was a change in the way that the pension was increased annually. It used to be the case that it was increased in line with the rate of increase in prices or average earnings, *whichever was the higher.* Generally, it is the latter which increase faster. In 1980, this double link was scrapped by the new Conservative Government and, since then, the pension has only been increased in line with prices. By 1997, this meant that single pensioners had lost £20 per week and pensioner couples had lost £30 per week (*The Guardian*, 18 July 1997). In 1979, the state National Insurance pension was worth 21 per cent of average male earnings; by 1997 this had fallen to 14 per cent, and it is likely to have fallen to only 6 per cent by the year 2040 (R. Kelly, *The Guardian*, 14 March 1994). This sounds a long way off, just long enough to be directly applicable to readers in their early twenties and below!

One result of this decline in the value of the pension was that the number of retirement pensioners on means-tested benefits to supplement their basic pension rose. By 1994, it was a third of all pensioners, with 15 per cent actually on Income Support (IFS, quoted by Hughes, *The Guardian*, 16 May 1994). The reason for saying *actually on* income support rather than *entitled to* is that 1 million of the poorest pensioners do not claim their benefit entitlement (Sally Greengross, Director of Age Concern, quoted in *The Guardian*, 18 July 1997).

Changes in pension provision for the retired, introduced in 1999, affect this calculation. Labour brought in a guaranteed minimum income for pensioners and, in the 1999 Budget, linked its level to the rate of increase in earnings, not in prices. This is not a link to pension levels, but it does mean that the means-tested top-up that some pensioners need will increase in line with living standards generally.

Pensions and the social division of welfare

Richard Titmuss (1958) coined the phrase 'social division of welfare' to describe the variety of ways in which welfare may reach the citizen. The idea is central to understanding welfare and pension provision in retirement. He outlined three approaches:

1 *State welfare and benefits.* This is the obvious type of welfare provision that most people think of first. In 1977, for example, an additional top-up pension was introduced for people who would go into retirement with only their basic National Insurance state pension to live off. This was known as SERPS or the State Earnings Related Pension Scheme. It was meant to help the low-paid, the irregularly employed and so on, many of whom are women. The value of this scheme was reduced significantly by cuts brought in by the 1986 Social Security Act, but it has now been superseded by Labour's pension policy changes announced in December 1998 (see p. 136).

   Retirement pensioners can claim various means-tested benefits to supplement their incomes, notably Income Support and Housing Benefit.

2 *Private or market welfare.* Both occupational pensions and private pensions have increased enormously in the postwar era. The rise of the occupational pension scheme was charted by **Field** (1981). He showed that 2.6 million people were in such schemes in 1936, 6.2 million in 1953, 8 million in 1956, and 11.1 million in 1961. However, these are overall figures that mask differences between men and women, differences between full- and part-time workers, and other employment-status differences. By 1995, 58 per cent of men in full-time employment, 55 per cent of full-time women and 24 per cent of part-time women were in such schemes (*The Guardian*, 18 July 1997)

Activity
Why do you think that there is no figure for part-time men? Use a textbook, *Social Trends* or the General Household Survey to find out the percentage of women employed full-time and part-time.

In the 1980s, the Conservative government encouraged the growth of private pensions, such as by subsidising people to opt out of their occupational scheme. In all, millions made this move, with up to 2 million doing so on the basis of misleading advice. (*The Guardian*, 19 September 1997.) The companies involved were faced with compensation claims reaching billions. Critics said that the scandal reflected a government too wedded to insufficiently regulated market forces.

3 *Tax allowance or fiscal welfare.* This includes all the various allowances that can be claimed against tax so as to reduce a person's tax bill. The number and value of these allowances vary over time with government policy, but one general comment is that they tend to give most help to those on high incomes (Cole, 1986). In 1991, tax relief subsidy to personal pensions came to £1.1 billion, an increase of 36 per cent on the previous year, mostly benefiting the middle class (Keegan, *The Guardian*, 13 January 1992). Those on the top rate of income tax can claim their tax relief on pension contributions at 40p in the pound, unlike those who pay tax at the standard rate.

RESOURCES IN OLD AGE

This section looks in depth at how people's resources in old age are related to some of the main social stratification variables in sociology: class, gender and, to a lesser extent, ethnicity. Two articles have been particularly useful in planning this discussion: Arber, 1989, and Ginn and Arber, 1992.

Class and the elderly

Changes in the position of the elderly, notably in pension provision and retirement patterns, have led stratification theorists to develop two quite contrasting positions on circumstances of the elderly and retired (Arber, 1989). These are:

1 *Proletarianisation theory.* In some ways, this is an unfortunate title. Some readers may take the use of the word 'proletarianisation' as automatically suggesting a Marxist view of the elderly. This would not be an accurate reading of the title. The crucial point about 'proletarianisation' is that its use is obviously metaphorical. The theory is not suggesting that the elderly are literally going to sink into the working class/proletariat; they have, after all, left the workforce altogether. The explanation of the use of the term is that – as in Marx's classic theory of the proletariat – it suggests that the position of the elderly will deteriorate over time. It argues that they will become increasingly characterised by poverty and the homogeneity of social and economic disadvantage.

2 *Labour-market continuity theory.* The value of the title of this theory – even if it is not very elegant – is that it directly indicates what it is arguing. It simply states that there are continuing, and significant, inequalities among the elderly based on their previous labour-market situations.

Whilst the former theory *seemed* to have Marxian connotations, the title of this second one definitely suggests a Weberian root. The first theory places emphasis on the singular inequality between the elderly and the rest of the population, whilst the second stresses the inequalities that exist between different sections of the elderly.

Points of evaluation: the evidence for labour-market continuity theory
That there is considerable inequality in old age, and that this is likely to continue, is well documented now. Arber herself reviews evidence of inequality among men who are entering retirement before the statutory age, and of the circumstances of men over the age of 75.

General Household Survey (GHS) data does not show a large class variation in *rates* of premature exit from the labour market. However, there are different, class-related *reasons* for this early departure, as well as different *circumstances associated with it*. Men in the professions are much more likely to *retire early* with a pension, whereas unskilled manual workers are much more likely *become retired* through unemployment and/or disability in their fifties. If the latter have a personal retirement pension at all, its value is much smaller.

The extent of premature exit from the labour market has increased considerably over recent decades. Table 20 shows evidence from the 1994 GHS.

Table 20: *Premature exit from the labour market*		
YEAR	% OF MEN ECONOMICALLY ACTIVE	
	AGED 55–59	AGED 60–64
1975	94	84
1994	74	50

As for circumstances in the later years of retirement, there is evidence that the class gap in income between lower working class men and upper middle class men is less than before retirement. However, the class inequalities that do exist are likely to remain because they are based on sources of income that will continue. These include occupational pensions and unearned income such as from shares or other investments. Information on the pattern of savings comes from the government Family Resources Survey (1995/96). This found that 34 per cent of single-pensioner households had no savings, whilst 20 per cent of pensioner-couple households were in the same situation. At the other end of the scale, 15 per cent of single-pensioner households had over £20,000, and 31 per cent of pensioner-couple households did also. Drawing the line at £20,000 means that inequalities within this most advantaged group cannot be analysed: some will have savings way in excess of this sum.

Another source of recent data on likely future inequalities among the elderly comes in research from the NatWest Bank. It has constructed a 'pensions index' looking at where the nation stands in terms of all the types of pension discussed above. It argues that 'a comfortable retirement' requires £180 per week. Table 21 shows what it estimates the population will actually receive, based on current patterns of provision.

Table 21: *The NatWest 'pension index'*	
LIKELY PENSION	PROPORTION OF WORKERS
£180 +	21%
£120–179	23%
£80–119	23%
Less than £80	33%

SOURCE: NATWEST BANK

The extent to which pension provision is linked to pre-retirement circumstances is demonstrated by data from the pension company NPI. Its research showed, for example, that 70 per cent of people on incomes between £6,000 and £15,000 were unpensioned. This contrasts with just over 20 per cent of those on incomes over £51,000 (*The Independent*, 16 December 1998). The same research showed a very strong correlation between the size of a firm and the degree to which its employees have pensions.

There is evidence that inequalities among the elderly widened considerably under the Conservatives from 1979 to 1997. The richest 20 per cent, saw their real income rise by 70 per cent. At the bottom end are the 5 million who are eligible for means-tested benefits, though only 4 million of these actually claim them (*The Guardian*, 18 July 1997).

Some inequalities reflect a cohort effect in that they stem from the period in which people were born and grew up. Thus, a report by Age Concern points to the baby boom in the 1960s, when almost 10 million babies were born. Many of these people entered the labour market in the 1980s, just as a recession and labour-market restructuring were making secure, full-time, lifelong employment much harder to obtain. The implication of this for their savings and pension contributions is only too obvious (Evandrou, 1997).

The evidence of large class and income inequalities at, and well into, retirement lends considerable weight to the labour-market continuity theory.

Gender inequalities in old age

One obvious difference between the experiences of men and those of women in old age is that there are more of the latter and they are in retirement for longer. This is because women live longer and, *at present*, qualify for their state pension at 60, rather than 65. (It changes to 65 in 2010.)

In their account of gender inequality in old age, **Ginn** and **Arber** (1992) do not look just at unequal access to directly material resources along gender lines. They also analyse gendered patterns of health and access to health or social care. This is because the quality of older people's lives, and their level of dependence, is shaped by all these factors, not just by access to money.

Gender and material resources in old age
Dependency can be demeaning: it can reduce power and status. This is why feminists have criticised women's dependence on men in traditional family structures. It is also of concern to writers on the elderly (Townsend, 1981).

What Ginn and Arber do is combine the gender focus of traditional feminism with the kind of age focus found in Townsend. Women experience a double dependency in old age. They are age dependent in the way that men are, but they are also often dependent on men in retirement. This is because of the gender gap in the availability of pensions, both private and occupational.

Divorce and pensions
The dependence of married women on their husbands' pension rights has become entangled in the complicated issue of how a couple's assets are dealt with if they divorce. With about 170,000 divorces per year, this is an important issue for the many women who lose out in this split. At present, pension values can be taken into account with other assets when property is divided on divorce, but the technicalities of this often disadvantage women. Alternatively, they can have part of their husband's pension 'earmarked' for them at retirement, but this disappears if they remarry or if the husband dies first. Labour is going to introduce pension-splitting at the point of divorce, but its April 2000 start date has been put back.

Car ownership
One important material difference in old age between men and women that Ginn and Arber highlight is the level of car ownership. Car ownership affects access to services such as leisure and health care, as well as levels of dependency and social integration and social exclusion. The authors cite research showing that about 50 per cent of older men had access to a car in their household, compared to about 33 per cent of women.

Gender and health resources in old age
That health and dependency in old age can be problems is so well known that this image of the old has become a stereotype, a separate and additional problem for old people to deal with. Most recently retired people are fully able to look after themselves. Nonetheless, health problems do increase with age. For example, **Giarchi** and **Abbott** (1997) draw on research which estimates that about 1 million older people in the UK will suffer from Alzheimer's Disease by the turn of the century.

It is not the generality of health problems in old age that concern us here but rather their gendered patterning. Elderly women are much more likely to be substantially disabled than elderly men, and the gap increases with age. As regards access to support in old age, Ginn and Arber point to the considerable rise in the percentage of older people living alone. One fifth of all elderly men and one half of all elderly women are in this situation. This is higher for women partly because they outlive their husbands. This pattern is repeated in the households of elderly people with severe functional disabilities. One half of elderly women with such difficulties live alone, compared to only one quarter of men with these disabilities.

Ethnicity and old age

In some respects, this is still partly an issue waiting to happen. The explanation of this statement is to be found in Table 22.

Table 22: *Age structure according to ethnicity (%)*		
ETHNIC GROUP	AGED 45–59/64	POST-RETIREMENT
All Origins	19	18
White	19	19
Total Ethnic Minority	14	4
Afro-Caribbean	20	5
African Asian	10	1
Indian	18	6
Pakistani	11	1
Bangladeshi	13	1
Chinese	13	3
African	12	2
Other/Mixed	9	3

SOURCE: JONES, 1993, USING LFS DATA.

There are two striking features to this table. The first is the enormous gap between the percentage of white people over retirement age and the same percentages for all other ethnic groups. The second is the much greater similarity between whites and the rest in the 45+ age range.

Now consider when this data was collected, and move on 10 years. The percentage in the post-retirement age range for the ethnic minorities will be much higher, especially for Indians and Afro-Caribbeans. Even so, fewer of these will be in the very old age categories of 75 or 85+. In short, extreme frailty and vulnerability in old age will still be mainly a white phenomenon. The growing percentage of retired people from ethnic minority groups takes us back to the labour-market continuity theory. Their circumstances in old age will reflect their different labour-market locations before retirement. (See pp. 24–26.)

One further point to note here is one which looks forward to the next section on caring. This is the growing evidence that caring agencies sometimes stereotype ethnic minority groups as having strong supportive extended families. Sometimes they may do, but a policy based on such an assumption is likely to be an inadequate one because it makes no allowance for the situation where such support is lacking (see Naseem Khan, *The Guardian*, 10 September 1997).

CARING FOR THE ELDERLY – HOMES, HOSPITALS AND HELPERS

Older people can usually look after themselves for all or most of their retirement years, perhaps with some support or assistance. Sometimes, however, frailty, disability or illness means that they require much more than occasional assistance. In recent years, the question of how to care for these older people who need support has often been posed as one of institutional care versus care in the community. This is a rather simple dichotomy but it points towards some of the issues that need exploring here.

THE BACKGROUND – FROM HOMES TO HOSPITALS, AND FROM HOSPITALS TO HOMES

The National Health Service (NHS) came into being in 1948 with the commitment to 'cradle to grave' health care free at the point of usage, ie the treatment was to be paid for out of taxation, not by charges. Since then, the demand on the NHS

THE GROWTH IN COMMUNITY CARE FROM THE 1980s ONWARDS HAS BEEN HIGHLY CONTROVERSIAL, WITH POTENTIAL BENEFITS OFTEN BEING RESTRICTED BY POOR FUNDING AND A LACK OF COORDINATION.

from older people has grown considerably, particularly in the number of older people who have become long-term hospital patients. Sometimes, they were primarily in receipt of social care, not of medical care or treatment as such. However, the boundary between the two kinds of care is very difficult to draw. Nonetheless, it formed the partial basis of the policy of shifting the long-stay care of older people away from hospitals to other forms of care. Survey research suggested that the number of beds in NHS hospitals for elderly people fell by 40 per cent from 1988 to 1993 (*The Guardian*, 5 August 1993). That same newspaper reported that, by 1997, 50 per cent of all long-stay nursing beds had been closed – the biggest change to the NHS in 20 years.

COMMUNITIES AND INSTITUTIONS – THE BACKGROUND TO COMMUNITY CARE

With some simplification, it is possible to argue that there were two general types of reason why community care was introduced as a policy for the elderly and others from the 1980s onwards. One was based on a critique of what institutions were seen to be like, and the other was based on their cost to the government, relative to the perceived costs of alternative forms of care.

The first critique is rooted in the kind of analysis of total institutions made famous by Erving Goffman, whose work had such a strong influence on social work and sociology (Goffman, 1968). His argument was that many institutions where people ('inmates') spend the totality of their daily lives – prisons, mental hospitals, residential homes etc – tend to have a range of features in common. These are partly based on the bureaucratic administration of people's lives that these institutions impose. Inmates become institutionalised, dependent on the routines of the home or hospital. Goffman characterised total institutions as 'forcing houses for the changing of persons.' By this, he meant that they had a major impact on the self-image and identity of inmates. The routines of the institution and their labelling effects can have great power. In the case of older people, the suggestion is that they partly became old by virtue of living in homes for the elderly, and not the other way round.

Clearly, many older people who went into homes or hospitals did not need to do so, and many had a far worse quality of life than they need have done. Having said this, there is also evidence that Goffman's critique can also be applied to those older people living in their own private homes. Here they may come under the routine supervision, intervention and regulation of local authority and health service bureaucracies. One former care worker with the elderly living at home describes many as apathetic and effectively institutionalised in the Goffmanesque sense. 'It is not bricks and mortar that define an institution but the manner in which an organisation behaves toward bodies in its care.' (Hilary Gavilan, *The Guardian*, 17 June 1992.)

Something else worthy of mention here comes in a report from a charity concerned with the relatives of older people in care. This looked at the links between residents and their relatives. The research was based on 100 homes and concluded that all but three needed to do much more to make relatives welcome and to break down the gulf of communication and understanding between staff, residents and relatives (Relatives Association, 1998).

The second factor explaining the community care programme, the cost of institutional care, was one that was of special significance to a government wedded to the view that state spending and taxation should be kept to a minimum. This New Right view of the minimal state was reinforced by another of the then Conservative government's ideological commitments, namely its view that the role of the family in caring for its members had declined and ought to increase. In short, it was seen as cheaper for old people – and others – to be cared for 'in the community', especially if this caring was done free of charge by the community. Feminist critics of the Conservative Government's community care policy, such as **Finch**, have argued that, in this usage, community is code for family and family is code for women.

Under the community care system introduced in 1993, local authorities have to ensure that people's needs are met after they are discharged from hospital. For many – probably hundreds of thousands – this care will be in a private nursing home. There are fees for this care whereas the NHS beds that the elderly were in previously were free. These fees are means-tested. The free NHS bed was a universal benefit; financial assistance with nursing home charges is a selective benefit. Capital assets are taken into account when calculating this benefit. In 1996, government guidelines stated that those with savings of less than £10,000 were exempt from charges; between £10,000 and £16,000, some contribution was required; and over £16,000, the full cost had to be paid by the resident. Many elderly people were effectively forced to sell their houses to pay for their nursing home fees.

There have been many court cases about who should pay for the various forms of care that the elderly sometimes need, and the legal situation became extremely complex.

In 1998, Labour set up a Royal Commission on Long Term Care. This reported in 1999, and one of its conclusions was that the costs of *nursing care* should be separated from residential and living costs. Nursing care should be free at the point of usage and the £16,000 means-test threshold just mentioned should be raised to £60,000. It will be interesting to see what happens to the Commission's recommendations, given the costs of these, estimated at £1 billion to begin with and £6 billion by the year 2051. If the recommendations are adopted, then some of the problems indicated here will disappear. There are, however, early signs that the government is worried about the long-term costs of the scheme. The reader should check to see what has happened on this matter.

Help at home

If old people are living in the community and need assistance with day-to-day care, several types of helper can be identified who may provide this care:

1 *formal care through state services*: this may mean from the NHS (free) or from a local authority (usually charged for, perhaps means-tested). In 1998, a report on degrees of social exclusion noted that social service provision to help older people live at home was worsening (*The Guardian*, 16 December, 1998).
2 *market-based care*: this may mean private agency staff, such as nurses or domestic helpers, paid for by the old people themselves, or perhaps by a relative. This form of care is expensive and only available to a select few.
3 *charities and voluntary organisations*: these may be responsible for helping out with delivering meals-on-wheels or such like. A report by the Volunteer Centre, a Home Office-funded organisation, expressed concern about the disproportionate reliance of organisations like the Women's Royal Voluntary Service on relatively affluent middle-aged women for this voluntary work. The problem here is the growing tendency of these women to return to employment and become less available for volunteer work (*Daily Telegraph*, 31 May, 1990).
4 *informal care*: this is predominantly from (female) friends and relatives. This is discussed in the next section.

Research data from the Royal Commission on Long Term Care shows projections of likely increases in care needs between 1995 and 2031:

- Numbers in residential or nursing homes will rise from 407,000 to 666,000.
- Those receiving domiciliary or home care services will rise from 517,000 to 804,000.
- Those receiving community nursing will rise from 444,000 to 717,000.

The costs of providing these services will rise much faster than the economy is likely to grow (cited in *The Guardian*, 31 December 1998).

Care in the family

The availability of care or support from one's family in old age depends on a range of factors. One common approach in everyday ideas about family life takes the view that this support depends primarily on individual, moral factors such as how committed or 'good' family members are. A further aspect of this approach is the assumption that family members are generally less caring than they used to be, that the family does not care for its (elderly) members as well as it used to. This is just one variant of the commonly-held view that the family is in decline.

Points of evaluation – the family in decline?

There are, however, a number of problems with this family-in-decline argument. Some account of these problems will help clarify the discussion about the extent to which informal caring does occur within, and between, families.

Vagueness and myths of a golden past.   The idea that the family is in decline is dogged by vagueness. In short, the concept of 'decline' has been either unclear or defined in different ways in different arguments. This problem is added to by myths of 'golden pasts' at often unspecified times in history. The social historian **Anderson** (1983) deals well with this, as does **Pearson** (1983) in a more general account of alleged family and moral decline, and of hooliganism.

The comparative method – a brief note.   When comparisons are made between two groups to test the significance of a particular variable, it is important to ensure that the two groups are as alike as possible except in the one variable being tested. In experimental research, this is why a *control group* is used. In historical sociology, experiments are not possible.

Historical comparisons – problems of data and demography.   In order to test the idea that families care for their elderly members less now than, say, in the nineteenth century, a direct comparison between the two periods has to be carried out. This is not easy. Obtaining reliable data about family support is hugely problematic now, let alone then. Another problem is the one of comparing like with like. It is impossible to make comparisons between nineteenth and twentieth century rates of family caring whilst all other variables are held constant. A major reason for this is that, in the nineteenth century, far fewer people lived to what we now call retirement age. When they did, they did not do so for very long. Three-generation families did exist, but there were fewer then than today, and four-generation families were very much rarer. The question of caring for large numbers of elderly for long periods did not exist in the way that it does today. Put at its simplest, this means that to compare the amount of caring for elderly people today with that of the nineteenth century is invalid.

The decline of the extended family – some mixed messages.   Another problem of clarity, or a lack of it, in the family-in-decline argument is the way that the concept of extended family is used in quite different ways. This is important because it is members of this family network from whom carers are usually seen as being drawn. Occasionally, the concept is taken to mean the extended family household, though this household pattern has never been a widespread norm in British society (Laslett, 1965).

Willmott's account of kinship in urban Britain (1988) suggests three other possible approaches to the extended family, depending on proximity and frequency of contact:

1   the local extended family where some of a family's wider relatives, such as grandparents, live in the same locality as them. This was the case with about 12 per cent of the population;
2   the dispersed extended family where kin are more geographically spread out but where significant contact is still maintained. Letters, visits, phone calls and mutual support at key times or events are all possible with this type of relationship;

3 the attenuated extended family where both geographic and social distance mean such contact is much rarer. This accounts for about half the population, though it is a shifting half because many people here are at that youthful stage of the life cycle when close contact with kin is often weakened.

Recent research suggests that factors like the rise in divorce have weakened the link across the generations, resulting in increases in health and emotional problems among the grandparents (Drew and Smith, reported in *The Guardian*, 12 September 1998). There is other evidence that this type of contact is in recent decline, even if it remains higher than some stereotypes suggest. This evidence comes from the large and representative British Social Attitudes survey of 1995. In 1986, nearly 60 per cent of people had reported seeing their non-resident mother at least once a week; by 1995, it had fallen to below 50 per cent. The same trend was shown in connection with non-resident fathers. See Table 23 for details on this current pattern.

Table 23: *Frequency of seeing non-resident parents, 1995 (%)*					
	DAILY	AT LEAST ONCE A WEEK	AT LEAST ONCE A MONTH	LESS OFTEN	NEVER
Mother	8	40	21	27	3
Father	6	33	20	29	9

Caring for or caring about?

Another concept that may seem straightforward but where some clarification is needed is the concept of 'caring'. **Finch** (1987) distinguished between 'caring for' and 'caring about'. People may not care *for* their older relatives, in the sense that they spend some considerable time looking after them, but may still care *about* them. Conversely, when someone cares *for* others, it may be for a variety of motives. They may feel that they want to, should do or have to, or perhaps that there is something in it for them.

Finch's analysis points to the highly gendered nature of both the feeling of obligation to care for relatives and the social pressure to do so, even where this obligation is not personally seen as legitimate.

Because women are culturally defined as people who care in our society, the decision whether to care for an infirm relative – and most particularly a decision not to provide care – is very different for a woman and a man in equivalent positions. Quite simply, men have many more available reasons which others will accept as legitimate for not providing such support.

Finch, 1987

Changing patterns of care?
Finch asks whether care for elderly relatives is being provided more or less than in previous years. She refers to many social changes that may be thought to have made such care less likely.

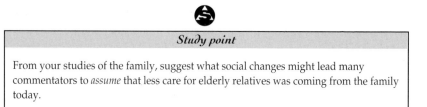

Study point

From your studies of the family, suggest what social changes might lead many commentators to *assume* that less care for elderly relatives was coming from the family today.

Despite factors, like the ones you may have just listed, apparently working to reduce the level of care available for elderly people within their families, Finch shows that such care does exist. Women, and to a lesser degree men, do provide much intra- and intergenerational care for the elderly in need. However, their ability and willingness to do this may depend on how much other support for them is available. A strong state support sector may be a necessary feature of strong family support, not an alternative to it. As an indication of the amount of this kind of caring, Finch cites research by the Family Policy Studies Centre. This shows that the financial value of all the care that people do for their elderly relatives is greater than the whole of state spending on health and social services for the over-75s.

Not so caring – the ill treatment of the elderly.
No sociological account of family life would be complete if it omitted reference to domestic violence. Similarly, no account of the lives of old people, whether living at home or in homes, would be complete without some discussion of their vulnerability to violence. They are vulnerable because of their low status and power (McNeill, 1988).

In 1989, the British Geriatric Society expressed its concern about the possibility of up to 500,000 elderly people being at risk of abuse, often in their own homes and often by their own relatives (*The Guardian*, 10 May 1989). Two underlying causes were suggested. The first is that the families looking after elderly dependent relatives at home get insufficient support for what can be an extremely demanding and stressful task. The second is that there is understaffing in hospitals and residential homes; and to this second point could be added inadequate training. More recently, a report has spoken about they physical and sexual abuse of older people running at up to 10,000 cases a month (Action on Elderly Abuse, 1996, reported in *The Observer*, 3 November 1996).

Community care – concluding comment

This account has obviously focussed on community care and the elderly. The general policy here has at different times, however, been concerned with a wide range of people whose lives have, perhaps unnecessarily, been spent within institutions. These include children in homes, prisoners and mental hospital patients. Clearly, each group has faced different problems with the policy and made different gains from it, and gains there often were, despite the criticisms and bad publicity.

Perhaps the most negative publicity, some would say sensational as well, has come over community care for the mentally ill. After a number of dramatic murder cases involving seriously mentally ill people released into the community, the government announced a major policy initiative in July 1998. This proposed a significant increase in constant supervision by 'outreach' teams and the building of special psychiatric units for patients causing most concern.

Two conclusions can perhaps be drawn from this announcement, one specific and one general. The specific one concerns the degree to which the previous community care policy for the mentally ill, at least implicitly, underestimated the care and security requirements of some of the patients who would otherwise be in hospital. This leads directly to the general conclusion, namely that the attraction towards community care as a cheaper form of care than residential or institutional care has led to the underfunding of the whole programme.

SUMMARY

- Old age, defined by retirement age, can last as long as childhood and youth but has been given much less attention in sociology.
- Filling this gap is particularly important in a book about wealth, income and welfare as all three are significantly associated with the ageing process.
- The issue of welfare in old age is not just one of income support or social security but also one of services and of social and health support. Central to the understanding of welfare in old age is an awareness of the economic circumstances and employment patterns of people before their retirement. Equally, the welfare of the elderly is strongly influenced by the level of support available either through statutory provision or informally from friends or, more likely, (female) relatives.
- The association between income and welfare, on the one hand, and old age, on the other, is significantly influenced by class, gender and ethnicity.
- Full understanding of class, gender or ethnicity is impossible without an understanding of old age.

STUDY GUIDES

Practice questions

1 'Age is at least as important a variable in social stratification as social class.' Critically discuss this statement, with particular reference to the socioeconomic circumstances of the elderly.

2 Critically assess the factors influencing 'the care of the elderly' in turn-of-the-millennium Britain.

3 Outline the demographic issues that sociologists need to consider when analysing the different circumstances of the elderly according to gender, class and ethnicity. Your answer should focus specifically on contemporary Britain.

(Question 3 could be treated as a question awarding 10 marks rather than the full traditional essay allocation of 25.)

Coursework suggestions

One of the issues discussed above concerns the role of the family in providing care for elderly relatives. There are a range of research topics which could be developed from this. These can be pursued through research at an individual level or through group work.

Select one of the following possible research topics related to this issue:

1 the nature and extent of kin contact across the generations;

2 whether people feel that care for the elderly should primarily be the role of the state or the responsibility of the family;

3 the extent to which family care should be provided more by female family members than by males.

For your chosen topic, draw up a hypothesis, or outline specific aims for research. Write a brief rationale outlining the sociological relevance of your study. Indicate what criteria for sample selection you might usefully follow in carrying out the research. Bear in mind issues like representativeness and the value of the comparative method. Outline what particular question areas would be most worth researching. Suggest any problems that you anticipate in carrying out the research.

5

POVERTY

Introduction

ALL THE OTHER chapters in this book cover issues related to poverty. However, there are a range of poverty-specific issues within sociology that need to be considered separately. One of the central issues is the conceptual one of defining poverty. Without a definition, there can be no satisfactory measurement, or indeed explanation. The poverty definition debate is not just a question of semantics, however. Nor is it a simple technical question solved by finding the 'correct' definition in a dictionary. Indeed, it is not a completely neutral, value-free exercise at all.

The task of defining poverty is a highly controversial one because it is closely bound up with people's personal values and ideological leanings. This can be neatly illustrated by two snippets from the press:

1 April 1996: the Conservative Secretary of State for Social Security, Peter Lilley, said that the Government would not be drawing up a national plan to eradicate poverty as agreed at a UN convention in 1995. The reason he gave was that such a strategy was unnecessary as there was no poverty in Britain.
2 April 1997, *The Observer*: 24 per cent of the population in Britain lives in poverty. These two reports do not mean that poverty increased, over one year, from zero to a quarter of the population. Rather, they show the implications of using two very different definitions to measure poverty.

Study point
Why do you think Mr Lilley would have argued against the existence of poverty?

Table 24: *Issues, concepts and authors and sources in this chapter*		
KEY ISSUES	KEY CONCEPTS	KEY AUTHORS AND SOURCES
Defining poverty; concepts and controversies	Absolute; relative; subjective; environmental poverty	Rowntree; Townsend; Mack & Lansley; Runciman; Galbraith
Changing extent, nature and distribution of poverty; explanations of poverty	Feminisation of poverty Life cycle of poverty Social excusion 'Work rich' and 'Work poor'; workless households Cycle of deprivation; culture of poverty	Pahl; Graham (including on children) Kumar Oppenheim; CPAG Murray
Ideology and poverty	Primary and secondary poverty The 'underclass'	Rowntree Murray; Mann

DEFINITIONS OF POVERTY

The solution to the definitional problem indicated above is not to try to say that there is one true definition but to look at a range of definitions and consider their respective strengths and weaknesses. Within sociology, there have been at least four main approaches to defining poverty. Here is a resumé of the central elements of each.

1 ABSOLUTE POVERTY

- The sociological roots of this approach are to be found in **Joseph Rowntree's** studies of York in the late nineteenth century, studies that were repeated twice in the first half of the twentieth century.
- Rowntree's approach was to work out the cost of maintaining 'minimum physical efficiency'. He was looking for the *cheapest* way of meeting the basic needs for survival.
- The dietary needs of people were calculated according to the newly developing science of nutrition, with allowance being made for gender and occupational differences in calorie needs.
- People who had incomes too low to meet these needs were said to be in *primary poverty*. People whose incomes did cover these needs but who spent their money unwisely or irresponsibly were said to be in *secondary poverty*.
- This distinction has often been used in the ideological construction of the 'deserving' and the 'undeserving' poor.

- Rowntree did recognise some elements of the social in his calculation, especially in his later studies, but kept such inclusions to the minimum for fear that his research would be considered too generous on the poor and therefore dismissed by critics.
- Rowntree's approach to absolute poverty was incorporated into the calculation of subsistence needs for National Assistance rates after the Second World War. This did not fundamentally alter as National Assistance became Supplementary Benefit (1967) and then Income Support (1988).

Points of evaluation – strengths and weaknesses of the absolute definition of poverty

- A major strength claimed for this absolute definition of poverty is that it is possible to make historical and international comparisons. This is because basic physical needs for survival are fairly constant between societies, and comparative rates of poverty are therefore based on comparing like with like.
- One problem with using the latest science of nutrition was that it was based on knowledge that the poor would not have. This problem of knowledge is still present today, and it is compounded by material problems such as not being able to buy at the cheapest prices. This is illustrated by the ease with which people with money can afford to buy in bulk, perhaps using a car, and put food in a large freezer. The poor have to buy locally in small amounts. They are also less able to economise on fuel bills by installing energy-saving double-glazing and so on.
- The very idea of seeing poverty as an absolute, unvarying over time and place, is highly problematic. This is because our very ideas of survival are social constructs; they are relative. In contemporary Britain, a death before 60 counts as a premature death, but most societies in history would not have considered it such.
- Perhaps the biggest problem with the absolute definition of poverty is that it treats people in predominantly physiological terms, ie as having needs which are defined around biological health and survival. Critics argue that people, as members of societies, have needs that go beyond survival. These needs may be defined by the roles they play in society, such as in the family, as well as by the cultures and religions of which they are members.

2 RELATIVE POVERTY

- The recent sociological root of this approach is to be found in the critique made of Rowntree by sociologists such as **Townsend**, but the idea goes back much further than this. Oddly, given how he is seen as an icon of right wing causes, it is **Adam Smith** who gives one of the earliest clear arguments in favour of poverty as social or relative.

> *By necessities I understand not only commodities which are indispensably necessary for the support of life but whatever the custom of the country renders it indecent for creditable people, even of the lowest order, to be without.*
>
> Adam Smith, The Wealth of Nations, cited in Oppenheim and Harker, 1996

- This definition sees poverty as specific in both place and time. What is poverty in one society may not be so in another. Similarly, within one society, ideas of what counts as poverty change over time.
- The focus of relative poverty is on the social expectations and obligations that society places on people. For example, there are expectations of being able to participate in the social rituals and activities that members of a society take for granted. Obvious examples include buying birthday presents for children and eating culturally prescribed diets, perhaps set foods for particular days or festivals.
- *Social exclusion.* A similar idea, associated with relative poverty and its emphasis on social participation, is that of social exclusion. After the 1997 General Election, Labour set up a Social Exclusion Unit. Its remit was to explore and propose policies to tackle the circumstances and institutions which exclude, which act as barriers to full social participation and integration – political, economic and cultural. First among its concerns were truancy and school exclusions, street homelessness and the plight of people living on highly deprived housing estates. This widening out of the approach to poverty issues risks a dilution of focus but has policy merits as well. It involves moving from a purely income-based approach to a multi-dimensional one, and from a focus on the individual to one on the community (Oppenheim, *The Guardian*, 1 April 1998). When he announced the setting-up of the Social Exclusion Unit in August 1997, the Prime Minister said:

> *This is about more than poverty and unemployment. It is about being cut off from what most of us regard as normal life.'*

This being 'cut-off', in fact, is what many sociologists regard poverty as being about.
- There is one aspect of the relative concept of poverty that is particularly interesting in terms of wider social theory. This is the degree to which the implicit theoretical underpinning of the idea can be seen to parallel some of the concerns expressed by **Tumin** in his critique of **Davis** and **Moore's** functionalist theory of social stratification. This critique pointed to the negative (ie dysfunctional) social consequences of social inequality (Tumin, 1953). These contrast with the positive (ie functional) consequences of inequality, emphasised by the previous Conservative Government.

Study point

1 What do you think the Conservatives saw as the positive social benefits of inequality?
2 Research Idea: consider how it would be possible to test the idea that conceptions of poverty change over time within the same society. To what extent would research on three different generations or age-cohorts provide the answer to this question?

Points of evaluation – strengths and weaknesses of the relative definition of poverty
Some of the strengths and weaknesses of this definition are simply the weaknesses and strengths of the absolute definition. However, two problems need to be particularly highlighted. One is the problem of operationalisation and the other is the difficulty of comparison.

Operationalisation
It is one thing to say that poverty has to be judged by the minimum standards or expectations of the day within in a given society. It is quite another to be able to say precisely what these standards are. Operationalising the concept of relative poverty is *at least* as hard as operationalising the concept of absolute poverty. Three different approaches to doing this are illustrated below:

1 A deprivation index.
Townsend attempted to operationalise the concept through a deprivation index of 12 widely shared, or approved of, lifestyle characteristics (possessions, aspects of lifestyle and diet, etc). He then correlated these with income. He found that exclusion from these characteristics was highly linked to income, and that below a certain 'threshold' income, there was a sharp and disproportionate increase in the their absence (*New Society*, 17 September 1981).

Piachaud strongly criticised Townsend's approach (*New Society*, 10 September 1981). He argued that some of the characteristics are more about taste or choice than poverty; for example, cooked breakfasts and eating meat.

Without doubt, there are different ideas about these characteristics within the population. Nonetheless, Townsend defended his position. He argued that there was a significant correlation between their absence and household income levels. In other words, the number not having them through choice was statistically less significant than the number not having them because they could not afford them.

2 What the public think.
Mack and **Lansley** have carried out two representative surveys of the population to see what possessions and lifestyle activities are considered necessities. The

surveys were seven years apart and did show the time relativity in attitudes to poverty referred to above. For example, in 1990, 15 per cent more of the population considered a fridge a necessity than did so in 1983: 92 per cent versus 77 per cent. Interestingly, the proportion defining a week's annual holiday away, not with relatives, as a necessity fell from 63 per cent to 54 per cent.

An absence of 'necessities' may be a result of a lifestyle choice, but the survey asked about this directly and took account of it.

Mack and Lansley defined poverty as the situation where respondents lacked three or more of the socially defined necessities *because they could not afford them.*

Activity

A research suggestion, to be carried out as a whole class or in groups, is as follows. Hypothesis: different age/class/gender/ethnic groups will define poverty differently. Draw up a list of possessions or activities which you think are household or family necessities today. Test out the list on different samples of the population. Each group, or each member of a group, could focus on a different type of sample. Alternatively, simply use Mack and Lansley's list for the research.

3 Statistical approaches.
This section looks at two ways of operationalising relative poverty using purely statistical calculations.

An early example was from another study by Townsend, along with **Abel-Smith**. In their book that was credited with rediscovering poverty in the 1960s after its supposed disappearance, they adopted a poverty line of 40 per cent above the social security level. Their argument was that National Assistance rates were that much below the poverty line. (Abel-Smith and Townsend, 1965). This approach was used in other influential poverty studies in that decade and beyond (see Coates and Silburn, 1970).

More recently, the Child Poverty Action Group and others have used average income statistics in defining and measuring poverty. Any individual or household receiving below half-average income is seen as being in poverty. For various reasons, housing costs are deducted before this measure is worked out. In 1995, for example, the poverty line for a family of two adults and three children aged 3, 8 and 11 was £196 per week.

The problem of comparison
What measures like the previous one allow is the ability to make comparisons over time or between different societies. Statistics can be produced showing

which countries have the highest and lowest percentages of their populations below half *their* average income. However, half-average income will, of course, rise, or fall, as average income does and this shows that, whilst comparative statistics are possible with this relative measure of poverty, these comparisons have their limitations. Like other relative poverty definitions, they are not *fully* comparing like with like.

3 SUBJECTIVE POVERTY

The idea behind this definition is people's perceptions of themselves. This has some surface similarities to relative poverty because these self-perceptions are usually based on people seeing how they stand *in relation to others*, comparing themselves with them. The group which is the basis for this comparison is called a *reference group* (Runciman, 1966). People may compare themselves to others in their own social world or group, but need not necessarily do so.

Points of evaluation – strengths and weaknesses of the subjective definition of poverty

- Perhaps the most obvious problem is precisely that this is a subjective measure. It is based not on a common standard that is applied to all but purely on how people define themselves. Two people on identical incomes and in identical circumstances may well define themselves quite differently: one may see herself as poor and the other may not.
- In this sense, it is not really attempting to make the same kind of measurement as the two measures of poverty considered above. So long as this is clear, the value of subjective poverty as a measure can be considered in a different light. It needs to be remembered that sociologists are not just interested in the structural elements of people's lives (jobs, money etc). They are also interested in how people perceive, define and make sense of their social worlds. Part of the reason for this latter interest was most clearly articulated by **W. I. Thomas**, an early influence in the development of the *interactionist* perspective in sociology. It was his argument that insofar as people define situations as real, they *are* real in their consequences. If people see themselves as poor, it will have implications for their self-image and quite possibly for their behaviour.

Study point
1 Give one reason why some people might define themselves as poor despite not having an income below the poverty line used in most definitions of poverty.
2 Give one reason why some people living on incomes below most definitions of poverty might not define themselves as poor.
3 One possible consequence of people *not* defining themselves as poor, despite being on low incomes, is that they might not claim the benefits to which they are entitled. Suggest one possible social consequence of a large number of people who *do* see themselves as poor, even if they are not poor by other measures.

4 ENVIRONMENTAL POVERTY

All the above definitions are primarily based on individual or household income – or on how that is perceived. These are best seen as issues of the private domain. This definition of poverty looks at public services and provision, such as public health and medicine, transport, education, social services, leisure facilities and so on. Even a cursory consideration of absolute and relative poverty would show that physical health and survival, as well as the ability to meet society's expectations of standards of living and participation, are highly influenced by such public services.

In the 1950s, the American economist, J. K. Galbraith, wrote of the growth of public squalor amidst private affluence (Galbraith, 1970). Forty years later, he wrote that:

in the time that has elapsed, the contrast between needed public services and affluent private consumption has become much greater.

Extract from UNDP Development Report, reproduced in *The Guardian*, 9 September 1999.

An interesting, related development here is the new Quality of Life performance indicator announced in late 1998. Rather than just relying on the growth in national wealth, as measured by gross domestic product, the Government announced a wide range of indicators of the quality of life. Many of these have nothing to do with poverty, but some do. The main ones here are housing quality and the level of social investment, such as in public health and transport assets, but others include education and training, employment and health. This is not a poverty measure, but it is likely to provide data which can be used in measuring public or environmental poverty.

Points of evaluation – strengths and weaknesses of the environmental definition of poverty

- Its greatest strength is that it targets the fact that the quantity and quality of life are shaped by more than just individual or household incomes.
- A particular problem is that it can be difficult to operationalise. This is partly because the absence of public services in an area will not affect all people living in that area to the same degree. Some will have access to alternatives, private medicine or transport for example, whilst others will not.

THE EXTENT AND DISTRIBUTION OF POVERTY

The extent and distribution of poverty, of course, will depend on the definitions used.
Most of this section draws upon research using relative definitions.
Several features of poverty in Britain in the 1980s and 1990s stand out:

1 One is the large increase in the numbers of the poor from the late 1970s onwards.
2 Another, related to this, is its increase relative to the rest of Western Europe.
3 The third concerns the changes and continuities in its pattern of distribution.

1 THE NUMBERS IN POVERTY

The debate about the numbers in, or said to be in, poverty has been a highly politically sensitive one ever since poverty was 're-discovered' in the early 1960s (Cole, 1986). More recently, a particularly contentious aspect to this debate has been a focus on the extent of the rise in poverty during the Thatcher and Major Governments from 1979 to 1997.

It is not surprising that commentators report a considerable rise in poverty over these years, given the social, economic and demographic changes that were occurring. These included:

- a huge, if fluctuating, increase in unemployment
- an ageing population
- a growth in the number of one-parent families
- an increase in the number of 'workless households'
- cuts in welfare benefit coverage or benefit levels for some groups
- a widening of income inequality, including an increase in the numbers on low pay.

The arguments about how much, if at all, poverty increased, points back to Peter Lilley's claim referred to at the beginning of this chapter: there is no poverty, he decreed!

'No rise in poverty under Mrs Thatcher'
Research on 80,000 men aged 25–44 commissioned by Peter Lilley, seemed to indicate that poverty had not worsened under Mrs Thatcher's prime ministership. First, it showed that only 16 per cent of the men in the bottom one tenth of the income scale in 1978 were still there in 1992/93. Second, there was the finding that 90 per cent of this bottom decile had seen a *real* increase in their earnings over the period, compared to only 75 per cent for all men. Indeed, more broadly, the bottom fifth of male earners had had a rise in real incomes of 42 per cent between the two dates, compared to 33 per cent for those starting in the top quintile (*The Guardian*, 27 June 1998).

'Big rise in poverty under Mrs Thatcher'

Data from the Department of Social Security (DSS) at the same time, however, shows that statistics can be selected and interpreted in different ways. In 1978, 5 million people lived below half-average incomes; by 1992/93, this number had risen to 14.1 million (*The Guardian*, 27 June 1998). On this definition, poverty had almost trebled.

Research also published that year pointed to a rather complex pattern of change in inequality and poverty. This showed that between 20 and 30 per cent of the population failed to benefit from the economic growth of the 1980s. (Joseph Rowntree Foundation, reported in *The Guardian*, 27 March 1998). This contradicts the so-called 'trickle down' theory of wealth creation popular with the government then. This argued that, as the rich got wealthier, so too would the less well off inevitably gradually benefit.

The same research also showed that there was a decline in inequality and poverty in the latter days of the Major government. This was apparently the result of a tailing off in the rate of increase in incomes of the well-paid and a one-off effect of the abolition of the Poll Tax which had hit those on low incomes the hardest. It is impossible to know whether the reduction in poverty would have continued had the Conservatives won the 1997 election.

According to one of the poverty measures referred to above and sometimes used by the Child Poverty Action Group, that of the proportion of the population living at or below social security level, there was a huge rise in poverty. That percentage increased from 14 per cent in 1979 to 24 per cent in 1992. On another relative measure, the percentage of the population on less than half-average incomes, there was also a big rise over that period. The figures rose from 10 per cent in 1979 to 24 per cent in 1995 (Family Expenditure Survey, *The Guardian*, 16 October 1998).

Study point

Using the evidence above, write a 100-word article, for a sociology magazine, that summarises the arguments about whether or not poverty increased under the Conservatives in the 1980s and 1990s.

2 THE EXTENT OF POVERTY IN BRITAIN –
THE INTERNATIONAL CONTEXT

The 1998 United Nations Human Development Report put Britain fifteenth out of 17 industrialised nations in 1995 on a measure of poverty based on an amalgamation of four different indices: life expectancy, deprivation in knowledge, deprivation in income and social exclusion. Fifteen per cent of the population were said to be in poverty. (*The Guardian*, 9 September 1998).

Another study, this time of the European Union, looked at the regional distribution of poverty in Europe. A region's poverty was defined as being where it had a gross domestic product (GDP) per head of less than three-quarters of the average throughout the EU. In 1995, only two regions in the whole of Northern Europe were amongst this poorest category. Both were in the UK: Merseyside and South Yorkshire (Eurostat Report, 1998, from *The Guardian*, 17 April 1998). However, there are problems with the way these regions are constructed and where the boundaries fall. Thus, in the 1999 Report from Eurostat, Inner London came out as the richest region in Europe. This is a reflection of the enormous incomes in the City and not of the affluence of Hackney or Tower Hamlets, in reality among the poorest areas in Britain. The report also showed that Britain had the greatest inequalities between its regions of any EU country, with four regions now below three-quarters of the average EU GDP (*The Guardian*, 10 February 1999).

3 THE DISTRIBUTION OF POVERTY

This section looks at ways of analysing the pattern or distribution of poverty. Traditionally, the distribution of poverty was considered in terms of the kinds of risk categories identified in the 1942 Beveridge Report: the elderly, the unemployed, the sick, families with children, and the low-paid. These effectively became the basis of claimant categories: the pension, unemployment benefit etc. These are different to the sociological concepts and categories that interest sociologists more, namely class, gender and ethnicity. Age and disability could be added to this list even though they are partially incorporated in Beveridge's categories as well. It is important to emphasise the social, rather than purely medical, dimension to disability (Davies, 1994). Table 25 nonetheless focusses more on just three of these variables: age, gender and class.

In real life, of course, people do not fit just one of the categories of class, gender, age or ethnicity. Categories of advantage and disadvantage intersect and sometimes reinforce each other. For example, working class women are likely to be 'doubly' disadvantaged compared to middle class men, and so on. Another example of this is found in an excellent study of the interconnections of ethnicity and child poverty, as linked to low pay, unemployment, family size and demography (Kumar, 1993).

Table 25: *Categorising poverty: sociological perspectives*			
CLIENT/BENEFIT CATEGORIES	CLASS/LIFE-CYCLE ANALYSIS	GENDER/FEMINIST ANALYSIS	AGE/DEMOGRAPHIC ANALYSIS
1 The elderly 2 The chronic sick and disabled 3 Single-parent families 4 The unemployed 5 The low paid	These five groups are not really distinct groups but are often the same people at different stages of the life cycle. It is the working class who are most prone to poverty through low wages or unemployment and in retirement. They are more at risk of chronic sickness and disability. They also have higher rates of divorce and single parenthood.	Women are more at risk of poverty in most of these five categories. Note particularly: more women live to, and well beyond, retirement; however, they also have worse pension provision than men. Single parents are mostly women, as are the low paid. Dependent wives are sometimes among 'the hidden poor'. The growth, or growing recognition of female poverty is referred to as 'the feminisation of poverty'.	The first of these categories is defined by age. The elderly as a % of the poor have declined with the growth of poverty elsewhere and with the growth in private and ocupational pension schemes. As regards the rest, the most significant feature of recent times is the growth of child poverty: children feature as the dependants of unemployed, low paid, sick/disabled and single parents. In 1993/94, 4.2m children in Britain were in poverty; ie one third. In 1979, it was one tenth (*The Independent*, 16 October 1998).

Ethnic diversity – the case of the Irish

One ethnic minority group that probably will not be in texts is that of the Irish in Britain. This omission points towards a general problem in the way that the concept of 'ethnicity' is used in most sociological texts, and in political and public debates. This problem is that the term is used mainly, perhaps almost exclusively, to refer to those ethnic minorities who have their ancestry in Africa or Asia. The large, white European ethnic minorities of Polish, Italian or Cypriot descent are hardly mentioned, though **Oakley**'s study of Cypriot family life in London is an exception.

In terms of the Irish *within* Northern Ireland, there is research showing higher rates of poverty in Ulster than on the mainland (Ditch, 1980; Evason, 1983). Interestingly, rates of poverty in that province vary according to religious affiliation. This was indicated by research on religious affiliation and patterns of educational achievement. In 1995/96, 45.1 per cent of children in Catholic secondary (modern) schools were on free school meals, one powerful indicator of social deprivation. In Protestant secondary (modern) schools, the figure was only 25.9 per cent. For grammar schools, the figures were 16.5 per cent and 2.9 per cent respectively, also indicating a strong class link with school selection in both religious sections of the population (*Times Educational Supplement*, 19 January 1996).

More recent material notes the 1991 census showing that the Irish (from either the North or the South) constituted the largest ethnic minority group by immigration in Great Britain, ie 1.5 per cent of the population (Commission for Racial Equality (CRE), 1997). It should be remembered that Northern Ireland is not part of Britain but is part of the United Kingdom. When the Irish born in Britain are added to their children, the percentage figure becomes 4.6, and over 11 per cent in Greater London. The CRE points out that there is little monitoring of the socioeconomic circumstances of the Irish in Britain, but research does indicate that most of the Irish-born population are in the most socially deprived occupational groups and have above-average unemployment rates.

EXPLAINING POVERTY

A central element in the sociological perspective is that social phenomena, like poverty, cannot adequately be explained at – or 'reduced to' – the individual level. This is not to say that everything can be explained sociologically. Psychologists and biologists have significant contributions to make in understanding many elements of human behaviour, more than some sociologists are willing to accept. Nonetheless, it is the contention here that these psychological and biological contributions are limited in scope, perhaps particularly in explaining poverty.

One of the problems with the explanations of psychologists and biologists is that they find it hard to explain major variations in the pattern of social phenomena between social groups and within the same social groups over time. Between 1979 and 1989, poverty in Britain more than doubled. This cannot be explained by individual factors of either the psychological or the biological kind. The same applies to changes in crime, divorce or educational achievement rates over time.

At a correlational level, it is possible to indicate the kinds of household that are most at risk of poverty. These are the people or households who are outside, or only partially inside, the labour market, and those who are within it but poorly rewarded for being so.

LOW PAY

Clearly, the latter issue just referred to is that of low pay, an issue already discussed in the general debate on income inequality. However, its specific link to poverty needs to be considered briefly as well. A 1998 article for the Employment Policy Institute by Dutch academic **Ive Marx**, cites data from the Organisation of Economic Co-operation and Development showing an association between low pay rates and poverty rates (cited in *The Guardian*, 22 February 1999). The nations with the highest poverty rates among people of working age were, perhaps not surprisingly, those nations with the highest rates of low pay, defined as incomes below two-thirds of the median. Interestingly, it was the Anglo-Saxon countries of Britain, Canada and the USA where low pay was the most widespread, and the European countries where it was least prevalent. These high levels of low pay cannot explain the whole of the difference in poverty rates between the countries concerned. However, this *is* partly accounted for by levels of labour-market participation – and exclusion.

LABOUR-MARKET PARTICIPATION – THE 'WORK-RICH' AND THE 'WORK-POOR'

Table 26 indicates the close connection between labour-market participation and household poverty rates.

Table 26 – points of evaluation
- This particular table does not show the full significance of the labour market for people's standards of living. It does not, for example, show how strongly the level of income and risk of poverty at age 60+ is influenced by the nature of labour-market participation before that age (see the section on old age, pp 77–79).
- Additionally, it does not show the *indirect* dependence of children on the labour market. This is an important consideration because many of the household types most at risk of poverty contain children: they are the group most at risk of poverty in Britain today. This has come about for three main reasons: widening income inequality generally; a change in the composition of

Table 26: *The risk of poverty, by economic status in 1988/89*	
ECONOMIC STATUS OF HOUSEHOLD	PROPORTION LIVING IN POVERTY*
Couple, both in full-time work	4%
Couple, one in full-time and one in part-time work	5%
Couple, one in full-time work and one not working	15%
Single in full-time work	4%
One or more in part-time work	26%
Head or spouse, aged 60+	40%
Head or spouse unemployed	69%
Other	58%

*POVERTY DEFINED AS BELOW 50 PER CENT OF AVERAGE INCOME, AFTER TAKING ACCOUNT OF HOUSING COSTS.
SOURCE: OPPENHEIM AND HARKER, 1996.

low-income households from the retired to households with children; and widening income inequalities among households with children, especially as linked to ethnicity and to lone parenthood (Graham, 1994).

Activity

In March 1999, Tony Blair made a public commitment to abolishing childhood poverty in 20 years. Assuming Labour is still in office when you read this – or even if it is not – obtain data, such as from CPAG, to see how far this promise has been fulfilled.

- A third point to make is that a sociological exploration of the issues dealt with in the table would consider not just the household categories themselves but also the way that particular social groups are represented within them. The question of children's representation has just been referred to; the way that class, gender and ethnicity are represented within the household categories is also of crucial significance.
- It is also important to recognise that the table is showing what percentage of each type of household is in poverty. It is not showing what proportion of total households are in each type. Additional data is necessary to throw some light on this issue. The 1997 Labour Force Survey statistics on the so-called 'work-rich' and 'work-poor' provide some useful data on this. They showed that there were some 24 million households in Britain, and also showed what percentage of these are in the different household types. Of this 24 million,

three-quarters contained at least one person of working age. Over half of these had all their adults in employment, but over one in six households had none (cited in Denscombe, 1999). An even more detailed breakdown of household types by the presence and number of earners is particularly revealing. Table 27 has selected only those households which contain couples of working age or lone parents.

It is possible to do some simple arithmetic with the figures in Table 27 to disentangle those households with children and those without: 37.5 per cent of households here have them and 21 per cent do not. Of those with children, 18.5 per cent have two earners and 5.3 per cent have no earners. The 1950s model of one (male) earner to support a family household was a stereotype but had some basis in reality. It has certainly been replaced now by a diversity of types of household, and this polarisation between work-rich families and work-poor families is one of the central sources of inequality and poverty in contemporary Britain.

Table 27: *Earners by type of household, 1991*	
HOUSEHOLD TYPE	% OF ALL HOUSEHOLDS IN THIS CATEGORY
COUPLES	
Dual earners with children	18.5
Dual earners without children	11.0
Sole earners with children	11.1
Sole earners without children	5.8
No earners with children	2.7
No earners without children	4.2
LONE PARENTS	
Working	2.6
Not working	2.6

SOURCE: ADAPTED FROM LFS IN DENSCOMBE, 1999.

Going beyond the correlational into the theoretical shows there to be many disputes about *why* such households as those shown are in poverty and why some are work-rich whilst others are work-poor. Everyone can see that having no job may cause poverty, but some will see this lack of employment as a reflection of the economy whilst others will see it as a reflection of the characteristics of the unemployed themselves. In short, and in the language of economics, some will see it as a problem of demand for labour and others as one of supply.

This simple distinction in approaches to unemployment points to a general distinction in theories of poverty. Very roughly, they can be divided into two general kinds: the structural and the cultural. The former focusses on the distribution of resources (income, wealth, employment, opportunities and so on) within society and how that impacts on people's lives. The latter looks to the lifestyles and values (ambition, work ethic, fatalism and so on) of those in poverty as the source of their poverty.

Table 28: *Cultural and structural theories of poverty*	
CULTURAL APPROACHES	STRUCTURAL APPROACHES
1 The cycle of poverty. This approach borders on an individual explanation rather than a sociological one. The suggestion is that poverty is passed across the generations by inadequate parenting. It was favoured by some Conservative politicians in the 1970s/1980s. 2 The culture of poverty. This is a more sociological version of the first approach. It suggests that the poor have a distinctive lifestyle and set of values, particularly concerned with short-term time perspectives on life and a sense of fatalism about it. It was put forward in sociological terms by **Oscar Lewis**. 3 New Right underclass theory. This is really an adaptation of the previous approach. It suggests that certain groups of the population have become welfare-dependent, undermining independence and enterprise. Welfare benefits are seen as too high and too easy to obtain. It is most specifically single parents who are said to be in this category. Sometimes, ethnic minorities are said to be disproportionately located here also. The theory is strongly associated with **Murray** in America and **Marsland** in Britain.	1 Marxism. This sees poverty as a direct result of the exploitation of the proletariat by the bourgeoisie. The terms under which workers sell their labour to the owners of the means of production are so unequal that poverty wages are inevitable. It argues that unemployment is an inevitable feature of an economic system out of human control. 2 Labour-market theories. There are many theories of the labour market that point to enduring patterns of income inequality that give rise to poverty. In sociological terms, these theories are often Weberian in origin, but some have been adapted to feminist perspectives, such as some versions of dual-labour-market theory. 3 Welfare inadequacies. This approach, associated with social-democratic ideology, points to the gaps and weaknesses in the welfare system. Welfare benefits are seen as too low and as bedevilled by problems of low take-up and the poverty trap. An example of its concern is its criticism of the decline in the relative value of the state pension. Advocates of this view would include Townsend and voluntary organisations like the campaigning organisation Child Poverty Action Group.

To some degree, these contrasting approaches are associated with differing ideological perspectives. Traditionally, those on the political Left would have focussed on structural issues and those on the political Right on cultural ones.

Table 28 contrasts these two types of theory through a range of explanations. Those chosen are illustrative rather than exhaustive.

Points of evaluation

- Sometimes, the transmission of poverty across generations is seen as a product of the limited opportunities in life that poverty brings, or situational constraints as they have been called (Liebow, 1967). This is a structural theory of the poverty cycle, not a cultural one.
- A recent article highlighted some of the assumptions underlying New Right underclass theory: 'Without work young men are regarded as dangerous. Without fathers who work families are supposed to lack role models. Without a manual working class job men fall into the class below; the underclass. Without a man who works to provide a "proper" role model, young women will breed a second generation who prefer public welfare to work.' All these assumptions are then rejected by the author as lacking sociological validity (Mann, 1995).

Apart from these specific comments, the relative merits of the above competing general approaches are dealt with throughout this book.

SUMMARY

- The definition and measurement of poverty are highly controversial, due partly to associated practical methodological problems and partly to ideological conflicts about what poverty 'really' is.
- The discourse of poverty is often linked to theories employing concepts that need separate consideration in their own right, such as 'underclass' or 'social exclusion'.
- The extent and distribution of poverty have been changing over the years along with changing economic and political circumstances. Two changes in the distribution of poverty pointed to by commentators in recent decades have been the feminisation of poverty and the growth in child poverty.
- It is not only definitions of poverty that are ideologically charged. Explanations are also. Put very simply, some explanations seem to 'blame the victim' (ie cultural theories) whilst others point to wider, external forces (ie structural theories).
- Patterns and explanations of poverty are closely connected to the material in all the other chapters in this book.

STUDY GUIDES

Practice questions

1 Some sociologists have referred to the feminisation of poverty. To what extent does the evidence of poverty in contemporary Britain justify such a viewpoint?
2 Critically assess the argument that childhood has replaced old age as the age category most vulnerable to poverty.
3 'The main problem with most definitions of poverty is that they cannot be used for comparative purposes because of changes over time and between different societies.' Critically assess this view.

Coursework suggestions

The discussion above, and that in the next chapter on welfare, shows the importance of understanding people's beliefs and ideologies for a full grasp of poverty and social welfare issues. One aspect of this was demonstrated in a 1977 European Community survey showing that British people were more likely to blame the poor for their own plight than were people in other European countries (reported in *Frontline*, the journal of War on Want, December 1977). Questions asked included asking people what they thought the main reasons for poverty were, such as laziness, alcohol, illness, deprived childhood. To some degree, this kind of research can be used to see how widespread the support is for cultural or structural theories of poverty.

Design a piece of research that explores this issue. You could consider the various pros and cons of doing a small-scale piece of qualitative research into attitudes in a particular group versus a larger, quantitative study including members of more than one social group. The research should give consideration to why the people holds the views they do.

6

SOCIAL WELFARE

Introduction

SOCIAL WELFARE IS simultaneously a simple idea and an incredibly complex one. Let us start with the relatively simple, as the complex issues will emerge throughout the chapter anyway! Social welfare is concerned with the way society acts to meet people's needs for care, support or maintenance. Strictly, of course, society does not act: people do, both as individuals and through social institutions. This issue is important because it raises the question of which people or agencies are responsible for delivering social welfare.

One answer to this question is that the family is and has always been one of the main ways in which people's needs are met, or perhaps are not met. Another answer could be that it is the state which is ultimately responsible for ensuring that people's needs are met, even if it does not try to meet them all itself. The tension between these two answers is a backdrop to nearly all the debates about social welfare dealt with in this book. This chapter deals mostly with state welfare provision of a financial kind, whilst the chapter on old age (chapter 4) also explores the role of the family in welfare and caring.

EARLY STATE WELFARE

Early state interventions in welfare for, and control of, the poor go back to the Tudor period in the early sixteenth century. However, the most significant developments did not come until the nineteenth century, when there were developments in:

- government action, such as the new Poor Law based on the workhouse, the growth of regulation, such as in work and employment, state educational provision, and so on;
- self-help (friendly societies, building societies and other 'mutuals');
- charitable and philanthropic activity, such as in housing projects for the poor;
- the beginnings of private welfare (insurance companies).

Table 29: *Issues, concepts and authors and sources in this chapter*		
KEY ISSUES	KEY CONCEPTS AND THEORIES	KEY AUTHORS AND SOURCES
The nature of state welfare; care and control The state versus the market	Universal and selective benefit provision Collectivism and individualism; market forces. Ideology Sexism	Spencer; Marsland, Jordan George and Wilding Golding and Middleton Wilson; Lister
The development of state welfare	Cash benefits; benefits in kind Citizenship	Cole. Beveridge Alcock Marshall; Lister; UN Convention on Children's Rights
Recent (postwar) developments in social welfare	Consensus and conflict Dependency culture. Social exclusion The poverty trap	Murray A. Walker and C. Walker The Child Poverty Action Group

The early twentieth century saw the arrival of the first basic state pension (1908), the beginnings of the national insurance system (1911) and the controversy over the means-testing of the 'dole' in the interwar depression. For more details on this early history, see Cole (1986). It was not until after the Second World War, however that what became known as the *welfare state* took on its current form.

1 THE POSTWAR WELFARE PACKAGE AND CONSENSUS

The Second World War precisely illustrates the sociological idea that it is sometimes the unintended consequences of social action that have the greatest impact on the pattern or timing of social change. There is little doubt, for example, that the position of women changed as an indirect result of their directly productive roles in the war effort. The war also produced the biggest spur to welfare reform this century. Titmuss suggests that the war produced a sense of shared social solidarity that broke down the pre-war barriers to social reform. This, implicitly Durkheimian approach, has been challenged by sociologists from an alternative, class-conflict perspective: that of Marxism. Their account suggests that the postwar welfare reform was just one part of 'a new sort of social contract' between capital and labour. In return for welfare reform and some industries being brought into public ownership (such as the railways), the trade unions and labour movement gave acceptance to the capitalist mixed economy and to the Western capitalist side in the Cold War (Hall et al. 1978).

Hall's account makes it clear that it is the working class which is seen as having got the worst of the deal. This is demonstrated by two metaphors in the book cited here. One is taken from **R. H. Tawney**. Suggesting that gradual reform of capitalism is possible, he apparently once said that it is possible to peel an onion layer by layer. The other is from the book's authors who argue that, 'it is not possible to skin a tiger stripe by stripe.'

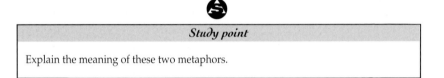

Study point

Explain the meaning of these two metaphors.

Definition: mixed economy

This is an economic system that is mainly capitalist, ie that is based on private ownership and the pursuit of profit, but where the state acts to regulate or modify the effects of the private market. One way it may do this is through ownership of certain industries such as the public utilities: gas, water and electricity.

Study point

What other forms does state intervention in the capitalist economy take, apart from ownership? Examples are found throughout this book.

The welfare package was based on the most significant social policy document of the twentieth century, the 1942 Beveridge Report. This report diagnosed what Beveridge saw as the five giant social evils of the time and laid out a blueprint of what should be done about them. The report was written in what now seems very old-fashioned language. The list of evils partly reflects this:

- want (ie poverty)
- idleness (ie unemployment)
- squalor (ie slums and the like)
- ignorance (ie poor education)
- disease.

All of these were the subject of government action either before the end of the war or shortly after. This book is not concerned to give details of the education (1944 Act) and health (1948 National Health Service) reforms. It does deal elsewhere with the long-term pattern of housing provision and tenure (see again pp 52–54). Here the focus is specifically on the economic and social policy responses to the evils of idleness and want. Unemployment is dealt with more fully elsewhere.

Full employment

Before the Second World War, an economist called Keynes had argued that governments could and should act to reduce unemployment. In Britain, his advice was largely ignored, but after the war, his idea that it was the responsibility of government to pursue economic policies that promoted full employment became part of the postwar consensus that lasted until the mid-to-late 1970s. A central part of his idea was that unemployment often represented a lack of demand , and that increased government spending, such as on public works or on welfare benefits, could increase demand for goods and services and thereby boost employment.

These policies were a direct and fundamental challenge to laissez faire. This theory, based partly on the writings of the eighteenth-century economist Adam Smith, states that the economy works best when market forces, such as the level of supply and demand, are not interfered with by government.

A modern supporter of Keynes's ideas, the economist Robin Morris, has recently argued the view that economic policy should aim to maximise the long-run growth of social welfare. By this, he means that it should seek to improve:

---

the average wellbeing of all in society, with disproportionate weight given to people with lower incomes, or those born with social, intellectual or material disadvantages.

(Morris, 1998)

Unemployment and the sociological imagination

The work of the late American sociologist C. Wright Mills perfectly indicates the above contrast between the two main types of explanation given for the mass unemployment of the 1930s: the individualist and the structural. In doing this, it shows how sociology can contribute to the understanding of social problems in general.

Mills uses mass unemployment to illustrate his distinction between 'a public issue of social structure' and 'a personal trouble of milieu' (Mills, 1970). The former can only be understood by looking to the historical circumstances, social forces and social structures which shape people's lives, such as the collapse of job opportunities that occurred in the 1930s. The latter is where only a handful of people experience a problem, such as unemployment; in these cases, it makes more sense to seek the explanation in that personal world rather than beyond it.

It is the task of the sociological imagination to show how people's lives and biographies – including the social problems that they may experience – are shaped by wider social forces, often unseen by those shaped by them. This is true, despite the fact that all of us are unique. This is why the generalised statement about social life that 'everyone is different' is true, yet extremely limited. Sociology takes us much further than that in understanding the human condition.

National Insurance, 1946

This widened an insurance scheme introduced in 1911, making it fully national and providing coverage for four of the five main 'risks' to poverty identified by Beveridge: unemployment, retirement, illness causing absence from work, and industrial injury. The fifth, associated with the costs of rearing children, was dealt with elsewhere.

Two of the central elements of the insurance scheme were that:

1   it was contributory, ensuring that there was no problem of entitlement, and no stigma attached to claiming, as was the case with the pre-war dole;

2   it was universal, meaning that it was not based on a test of income but was available to all in the relevant insured category: the sick, injured, retired or unemployed.

Family Allowances, 1946

These were introduced to help with the extra costs involved in raising a family, but initially were only for second and subsequent children. A child tax allowance already existed, but because fewer workers then earned enough to pay income tax, this only benefited higher earners. These would have been men/husbands, whereas the family allowance was paid to the mother.

When the two benefits were effectively merged in the 1970s to become Child Benefit, determined campaigns by feminist groups and others pushed the government to abandon its plan to pay the new benefit to the fathers.

Central features of the Family Allowances system were:

* its universalism; all mothers entitled to receive it

- its non-contributory principle. This did not produce any problem with entitlement rights as these were deemed to come through the simple fact of motherhood, and from a broader notion of *citizen* entitlement.

National Assistance, 1946

This was basically a safety net to ensure than no one fell through the welfare net into poverty, though it was not available to those in employment. National Assistance had the following characteristics:

- It was means tested and non-contributory.
- Benefits were set at what was considered subsistence level.

Points of evaluation – gaps and problems with the postwar welfare package

The extent of the reforms should not be underestimated. Even the Marxist **Miliband**, described them as:

> *a major, it could even be said dramatic, extension of the system of welfare which was part of the 'ransom' the working class had been able to exact from their rulers in the course of a hundred years.*
>
> Miliband, 1969

Nonetheless, there were gaps and problems from the outset, and others emerged over time. The main ones were as follows:

- *Women.* It was assumed in the Beveridge Report that married women would only partly and temporarily participate in the labour market. The Report stated that

> *In the next thirty years housewives as Mothers have vital work to do in ensuring the adequate continuance of the British race and British ideals in the world.*
>
> Quoted in Wilson, 1977

Their National Insurance contribution, when at work, could be a reduced one ('the married women's stamp'), insuring them only against industrial injury. For other benefits, the woman would qualify through her husband's contributions, reinforcing the ideology and reality of female dependence on men. As regards women as lone parents, Beveridge could not have predicted the rise in divorce and unmarried motherhood that occurred later in the postwar years. Other than for widows, his scheme made no real provision for women bringing up children on their own. These women had to rely on National Assistance.

- *People with disabilities.* People who were born with disabilities such that they could never work were unable to build up a contribution record for National Insurance benefit entitlement. Unlike those who sustained serious injuries at work, for example, they would then have had to depend on means-tested National Assistance.

- *National Insurance benefit levels.* These ended up being set below subsistence level, and consequently, many people had to turn to National Assistance as a supplement to their pension or unemployment benefit.
- *Benefit entitlement.* In contrast to sickness benefit or the retirement pension, unemployment benefit was for 12 months only. After that, the claimant would have to apply for National Assistance.

The postwar welfare package – some general observations
Citizenship

- *Citizens all?* One interesting perspective on the Beveridge proposals is provided by Marshall's citizenship thesis. His argument is that the struggle for citizenship rights has gone through three main stages. The first was concerned with civil rights, free speech, the rule of law and so on. The second was about political rights, such as voting and the right to stand in elections. And the third, were the rights to social and economic security. For Marshall, the fact that these rights were enshrined in the insurance system which provided benefits according to the principle of universality was confirmation that welfare was for all citizens, not just for the poor. Such a system of welfare is sometimes called *institutional*, in contrast to a system designed just for the poor which is sometimes described as *residualist*.
- *Citizens male? Citizens white?* Feminists see Marshall's ideas on citizenship to be partial. One critic argues that the system of giving social citizenship through National Insurance 'was predicated on the assumption of married women's dependence (Lister, 1989). Indeed, this has already been noted. More generally, **Lister** argues that Marshall overfocussed on issues of class and social citizenship and neglected 'other important determinants of social position, in particular race and gender'.
- *Citizens adult?* Elsewhere in her article, Lister refers to the question of children and citizenship, and it is worth picking up on some significant developments here since that article was published. In 1992, the British government ratified the United Nations Convention on the Rights of the Child. Two of the rights involved are particularly relevant here. Article 26 refers to the right of the child 'to benefit from social security', and Article 27 refers to 'the right of every child to a standard of living adequate for the child's physical, mental, spiritual, moral and social development' (UK Agenda, 1994). How much the government of the day kept to its commitments under the Convention is highly questionable. The point here, however, is to recognise how important it is not to stop the debate about rights and citizenship just when men have achieved these.
- *Citizenship and progress.* There is one other, primarily theoretical, issue that needs to be considered with Marshall's citizenship thesis. This is the danger

that such accounts of welfare, or whatever, read as if 'progress' is an historical inevitability, produced or rather revealed like a carpet being rolled out to display its colour and pattern. Whilst some other histories of welfare are much more guilty of this than Marshall's, all such accounts are flawed. There are two fundamental reasons for this. First, there are no laws of history (Popper, 1961). Second, what one person considers progress, another considers regression. Indeed, this is why it is better to keep value judgements in sociology under control: they usually say more about the sociologist than they do about society.

Of course, values and beliefs pervade the whole area of welfare and poverty. Perhaps here, there is a case for arguing that sociological studies can, and should, be value-relevant but not too shaped by value judgements (Barker, 1989).

Re-Distribution

There has been much discussion about the extent to which the 1940s welfare reforms were redistributive from rich to poor. The general trends in the distribution of income and wealth are dealt with elsewhere, but a few observations are required here also.

- Because Family Allowances and National Assistance were financed out of general taxation, and the tax system was reasonably progressive then, there was some vertical, downward redistribution. It is worth noting that the number of people incorporated into the income tax system had been 3.8 million in 1938/39, but that, under the combined impact of war and welfare spending, it rose to 14.8 million in 1948/49. This is still well below the 25.2 million it had become by 1988/89, a rise which cannot be accounted for by population growth or by the ending of the taxing of married couples as one entity in the 1980s (*The Guardian*, 22 September 1998).

- In addition to this, the nature of some of the benefits ensured some egalitarian redistributive effect. For example, the recipients of National Assistance would all be on low incomes, and their receipt of National Assistance would therefore produce some downward redistribution.

- However, things were different in the case of National Insurance. Because this was initially levied at a flat rate, ie the same amount was taken from all people regardless of income, it was clearly not going to shift resources from the rich to the poor. What it was doing was redistributing income across the life cycle, from times of health and employment to times of sickness, unemployment or retirement. This is horizontal redistribution.

WELFARE IDEOLOGIES

In order to understand fully the postwar reforms, and indeed the whole history of state welfare, it is necessary to explore the theories, ideas and beliefs that underpin that history and the various critiques of it. In practice, the difference between a theory and an ideology is hard to draw and may sometimes depend on the side one is on! Nonetheless, a simple distinction between the two is that theories are generally more inclined to the explanation of social phenomena, whereas ideologies are more concerned to condemn or legitimise them.

Many accounts of welfare ideologies start with the original categories suggested by **George** and **Wilding** (1976). Although their categories have been criticised and, indeed, have been amended by themselves over time, they are still a useful starting point. Table 31 draws on their work, as well as that of **Alcock** (1996), but not for all its inclusions or comments. Although the table puts the ideologies in boxes, in reality they are not completely distinct. Rather, they can *sometimes* be seen in terms of a continuum, such as in their attitudes to the state and so on. In other respects, these ideological outlines are best understood as Weberian ideal types (Collins and Makowsky, 1972).

In many ways, the reluctant collectivists and the Fabians (or social democrats) have more in common with each other than do any other two approaches, and indeed, their shared assumptions formed the basis of the postwar consensus between the main political parties in Britain from the 1940s to the 1970s. In addition, some Marxist critiques of market forces have much in common with Fabian or even Keynesian ones; see, for example, **Hobsbawn's** attack on unregulated market forces at the national and the global level (*Marxism Today*, October 1998).

Points of evaluation – problems with this ideological schema
Apart from the connections and points of similarity referred to above, there is a range of problems in applying this schema today.

- There is no reference to feminism. Hopefully, the experience of studying A level Sociology will have sensitised students to the way that many accounts of society render women invisible. The table here is no exception, though the diversity of feminisms might make it difficult to create a singular set of attitudes with enough in common with each other. Nonetheless, all feminisms *would* point to the sexism often found in the provision, or lack of provision, of state welfare; and in this, they could be treated as reasonably singular. In their more recent discussions of welfare ideologies, George and Wilding do include both feminism and greenism (see below) (George and Wilding, 1994).

Table 30: *Welfare ideologies and commentaries*			
WELFARE IDEOLOGY			
ANTI-COLLECTIVISM	RELUCTANT COLLECTIVISM	FABIAN SOCIALISM	MARXISM
Synonyms or related ideas/ theories	Market/neo liberals New Right Laissez faire Individualist.	*The Middle Way* (book by Tory PM to be, Macmillan, 1938).	Social democracy – perhaps an easier and more useful term to remember.	Critical theory.
Key thinkers/ advocates	Social scientists: Hayek, Marsland, Murray, Friedmann. Politicians: Joseph; Thatcher.	Beveridge Economist: Keynes (Both above – Liberals) Politician: Butler (Tory)	Social scientists: Titmuss; Townsend; Tawney. Politicians: Crosland, Hattersley (Labour).	Social scientists: Miliband, O'Connor, Saville, Wilson.
Political location Very approximate – for 'mapping' purposes rather than sociological understanding as such.	Originally, rightwing, and then mainstream of Conservative Party from mid-1970s. Rightwing pressure groups and 'think-tanks'.	Mainstream Conservatism until mid-1970s, then mainly from 'One Nation' sections of the party. Some 'Centrists' from other parties – as above.	The Labour Party until 1990s (?), especially its non-Marxist left. May have been replaced by notions of so-called Blairite 'third way'	Marxist academics (the number who use this self-label has declined). The former Communist Party, now Democratic Left. Leftwing groups.
Attitude to Income/Social Inequality	Necessary and desirable – provides incentives for 'wealth creators' from whom everyone gains. Inequality is about freedom to benefit from own efforts.	Necessary but only so far; extreme inequality leads to wastage of talent and to social disharmony.	Undesirable; inequality leads to wastage and is morally unjust; complete equality not practically sought; poverty restricts freedom.	Inequality seen in terms of class: class which owns the means of production exploits the employed class. Other forms of inequality flow from that.
Attitude to Market Forces	Highly positive – the economy is self-regulating. Prices, wages and employment will find their 'natural' level if left alone. Market forces reflect the freedom of the individual to choose.	Market forces and the capitalist system are fully but conditionally supported – market forces alone may lead to slumps and to extremes of inequality.	Market forces accepted to a degree, at least in the 'medium term'. Market forces based on supply and demand cannot fully meet people's needs; demand only reflects income/ wealth, not needs.	Capitalist market forces replace human decision-making with obedience to the laws of competition. Both the proletariat *and* the capitalist class are alienated. So-called free wage labour is really 'wage slavery'
Attitude to the State	A minimal, or 'night-watchman', state is preferred. The state as monopoly is seen as a threat to freedom. State interference makes things worse, through unforeseen consequences of its action.	State action is necessary to iron out problems of the market. Very sceptical of excessive state power: Europe's dictatorships of the 1930s/1940s made people wary or excessive state power.	The state seen as a potential force for good in society; NB role of well-intentioned, academic or administrative experts. Support for reform from above to make society more just and efficient.	The state is a class institution promoting capitalis/ruling-class interests. Marxists have varying views of the mechanisms and extent of this class dominance, eg on working class 'concessions' or 'victories'.
Attitude to State Welfare	Undesirable – (i) prefers individual/market welfare solutions; (ii) State welfare restricts free individual choice and creates a tax burden on the economy; (iii) Welfare benefits generate a culture of dependency; they should be means tested.	Necessary – (i) the market produces slumps and poverty which threaten social cohesion, and is economically wasteful; (ii) welfare spending is also a way of boosting aggregate demand to stimulate the economy.	Desirable (i) for tackling poverty and as a way of reducing social inequality; (ii) tax to fund welfare should be progressive and vertically redistributive downwards; (iii) benefits should be universal and based on citizenship.	Highly ambilvalent – state welfare is seen as (i) promoting the forces of production (a healthy workforce); (ii) legitimising the relations of production (NB ideology); (iii) a means of social control. Working class welfare 'gains' are often defended against government 'cuts'.

- There is too much of a focus on old politics and ideologies. This also is, of course, the claim of feminism, and there are other movements and campaigns too that, like feminism, do not fit into the old categories. These include environmental campaigns and groups. Their arguments tend to broaden out the concept of welfare, sometimes putting human welfare lower down the priority scale than traditional political ideologies do. Although their concern, therefore, is not welfare reform as it is discussed here, it has been noted that:

> *green ideologists argue that current welfare protection is based on the continuation of forms of economic growth that are unsustainable in the world in the longer term because of their economic destructiveness.*

Alcock, 1996

This green perspective is illustrated by the some of the responses to the government's decision to supplement economic growth statistics with measures of redistribution and quality of life. This was welcomed by the New Economics Foundation, an organisation that has sought to use its Index of Sustainable Economic Welfare to consider the relationship between economic growth, poverty, unemployment, unpaid work and crime (*The Guardian*, 11 November 1998).

Another example of green ideologies directly impacting on welfare issues has been with the setting up of an alliance of radical countryside and environmental groups to take direct action to highlight the number of empty houses, particularly those in towns. The aim of this group, Community Action on Empty Homes, is to prevent what it sees as unnecessary building development for new dwellings on rural land, with its attendant cost to the environment (*The Guardian*, 15 February 1999).

Finally in this section, a letter from Executive Director of Friends of the Earth to the *The Guardian*, praising some elements of the 1999 Budget, gives further illustration of green welfare and economics concerns. Charles Secrett welcomes the way that some tax changes have penalised heavy polluters and given money to industries that use environmental and renewable energy. (*The Guardian*, 11 March 1999).

- Ideologies are outdated. This claim was strongly argued in the 1950s and 1960s by American sociologists such as **Lipset** and **Bell**. Ironically, one of the reasons why ideology was said to be coming to an end was because of the very success of welfare reforms, the mixed economy, the acceptance of workers' rights and so on. These had supposedly transformed capitalism into 'welfare capitalism', or even post-capitalism. The convergence thesis argued that this process would inevitably lead all societies along similar paths, reducing still further the basis of structural and ideological conflict. Suffice it to say at present that, not long after these arguments were published in the

1960s, America and Britain experienced intense forms of political and ideological conflict. The 'end of ideology' was at least postponed.

The argument returned, however, in the 1980s and 1990s with the end of the Cold War between Western capitalism, on the one hand, and the former Soviet Union and Eastern Bloc countries with their official ideology of Marxism on the other. One American writer, **Fukuyama**, went as far as to talk of 'the end of history' (Cole, 1990a).

On this same argument, post-modernism claims that ideologies and theories that claim to answer the big questions of history and meaning are themselves part of history. There are no more grand narratives or 'big stories', just a plurality of representations and accounts of reality. This is not the place to go into post-modernism, but one criticism of it, often levelled at other types of relativistic argument too, is worth noting. This is that arguments which deny the existence of general truths are themselves staking a claim to general truth. Other than this, the view of Alcock is again worth noting. He accepts the post-modernist view that much has changed in the late twentieth century, including changes to traditional ideologies and structures of inequality. However, he sees such flux or change neither as completely new nor as leading to the end of ideological conflict.

THE END OF THE POSTWAR CONSENSUS – THE NEW RIGHT AND BEYOND?

This section looks at the re-emergence of ideological conflict in postwar Britain. By the mid-1970s, the political and welfare consensus was beginning to break down.

1 THE DECLINE OF UNIVERSALISM IN WELFARE PROVISION – PROS AND CONS

The gaps and problems in the postwar welfare package meant that the numbers of people dependent on means-tested benefits, like National Assistance, turned out to be far greater than **William Beveridge** anticipated. These numbers grew, and by the 1980s, piecemeal additions to the welfare system had reinforced this trend considerably.

Points of evaluation – the advantages of means testing
To Conservatives and other supporters of this type of benefit, its merits were many. First, means testing was said to ensure that people receiving benefits really needed them. Second, by targeting resources, it could either give more help to the really needy or save public expenditure by not giving money to those who did not need it. The latter option makes it possible to reduce the burden on taxpayers, thus reducing the risk that public tolerance of welfare spending will be

undermined. It also ensures that more money is left in the hands of those deserving it, thus maintaining the incentive to work and/or invest.

Two of the main means-tested benefits to be introduced in this period were as follows. Since the 1960s, rebate schemes to help those on low incomes with rates or rents had been in existence separately. In the early 1980s, they were integrated into Housing Benefit. In 1970, a new type of benefit was introduced which entitled those in low-waged, full-time employment to claim social security to top up their incomes. This was called Family Income Supplement (renamed Family Credit in 1988 and then Working Families Tax Credit in 1999). For a fuller summary of the advantages of means testing written by one of its leading exponents, see Marsland (1989).

Points of evaluation – the disadvantages of means testing

Although many millions of people and their dependants qualified for, and claimed, these benefits, critics of means testing pointed to the following problems. First, there is the problem of low take-up. Department of Social Security figures in 1995 showed that up to £3 billion in benefits went unclaimed in 1993/94. For example, one third of the 6 million people entitled to Council Tax Benefit did not claim it. And between a quarter and a third of pensioners did not claim their right to Income Support to supplement their pensions.

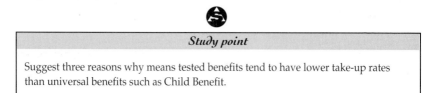

Study point
Suggest three reasons why means tested benefits tend to have lower take-up rates than universal benefits such as Child Benefit.

Another problem with means testing is what is known as the poverty trap. This is very simple to diagnose and very hard to solve. If people under a certain income qualify for means-tested benefits, then if their income rises, they lose some or, rarely, all of that benefit and may become little or no better off. The decline in their benefit entitlement as income rises is called the *taper*. Sometimes, there is a marginal loss of over 100 per cent; in other words, for each extra pound earned, there is a loss of *more* than a pound in benefit entitlement. This can obviously act as a massive disincentive to work or to improve one's position.

The problem of the poverty trap is recognised across the ideological divide in social science and politics. Few, however, have gone as far as New Right economist Professor Minford, in proposing a solution to it: no state benefits! He says that this is:

the rule in most Far Eastern countries, where people are expected to save and insure their families throughout their lives. As a result, savings rates are high, tax rates are low and there is no dependency culture.

Daily Telegraph, 13 October 1997

He does say, however, that withdrawal of benefits could only be gradual.

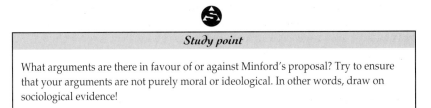

Study point

What arguments are there in favour of or against Minford's proposal? Try to ensure that your arguments are not purely moral or ideological. In other words, draw on sociological evidence!

A third criticism of means testing as the supposed solution to the problem of poverty is the fact that it sometimes simply does not always work in practice. Department of Social Security (DSS) statistics show that means-tested benefits as a proportion of all spending on benefits rose from 16 per cent to 35 per cent between 1979 and 1994/95. However, the share of benefit spending received by the bottom one fifth of the population fell from 43 per cent to 30 per cent over this period (cited by Lister, *The Guardian*, 23 January 1998).

For an account of means testing written by one of its leading opponents, see Jordan (1989).

2 THE END OF THE CONSENSUS — WELFARE CRISIS? WELFARE BACKLASH?

The policies brought in by the Conservatives after Mrs Thatcher became Prime Minister in 1979 have been variously described as New Right or simply Thatcherite. The different connotations of each label, or of other labels, need not concern us too much here. What is important is to get a picture of what this change of government and outlook meant for welfare issues.

The heading above points to two related ways in which welfare policies and perspectives have sometimes been characterised. Both are also connected to the growing tendency for welfare discourse in the mass media and right wing circles to centre on three interconnected definitions of state welfare: the fraud model, the burden model and the dependency culture model.

The fraud model

In the mid-1970s, cases of social security fraud were given an increasingly high level of attention in the popular and Conservative press. The stories focussed particularly on those claimants of unemployment or sickness benefit who, allegedly, really had work or were quite fit enough for it. The highly selective and stereotypical reporting of these cases had many of the elements of a moral panic. Stories of abuse far outnumbered stories about the low level of benefits or the low rate of take-up for many of them (Golding and Middleton, 1978). This is despite evidence indicating that underclaiming was widespread (Cole, 1986).

Significantly, one small piece of research carried out by the Policy Studies Institute for the DSS on claimants suggests that some of those committing social security fraud see it as necessary to support their children. They see it as preferable to 'real crime' and, interestingly, less serious than income tax or VAT fraud (*The Guardian*, 8 July 1997).

Research Hint

For anyone considering doing media research for a project or personal study, whatever the topic, it is worth having a look at the way **Golding** and **Middleton** used content analysis for their study. The scale of their research is not replicable at A level, but some of the problems of story or item categorisation in content analysis are well illustrated in their work.

By the 1980s, attacks on the unemployed had become less widespread, perhaps because there was some recognition of the difficulty of finding work in a recession. The abuse discourse was maintained, however. The popular press and Conservative politicians attacked young women for allegedly getting pregnant in order to get benefits and council housing. Although not illegal, this was characterised as immoral and manipulative and was part of a wider moral panic about the growth of the one-parent family. This attack on one-parent families reversed the trend for most of the earlier part of the century when the economic and cultural climate for such families had been gradually improving.

Many analysts accept that there is fraud, though estimates of the amounts vary widely. In March 1998, it was officially suggested the sum could be £4 billion. By July 1998, it was officially estimated at £7 billion.

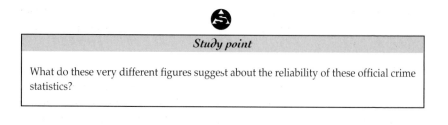

Study point

What do these very different figures suggest about the reliability of these official crime statistics?

The burden model

This is the idea that spending on the welfare state has grown so much that it is no longer possible to sustain it. The growth has long-term elements – longer life expectancy, leading to more pensioners – as well as ones that are more recent – more unemployment in the recession, and a growing number of single-parent families over recent years as well. The high tax cost of meeting these claims was said to undermine the public's willingness to pay for them. The tax burden was also said to be a drain on the productive economy; the argument here is that benefits are used for spending (consumption), whereas the money could otherwise be used more productively (investment). One leading right wing exponent of this view said:

High tax weakens entrepreneurialism and welfare weakens the resolve to work.

Skidelsky, cited in *The Independent*, 22 May 1997

Interestingly, some Marxists also saw a growing crisis of public spending in the 1970s. **O'Connor**, for example, argued that a contradiction existed within the modern capitalist system. On the one hand was the need to spend money on welfare to legitimise the system. On the other hand was the need to keep government spending down, and with it, keep down the tax on profits and personal incomes (cited in Mishra, 1981).

The validity of the burden model of welfare is evaluated elsewhere with particular regard to the ageing population (see pp. 72–73), but some observations can still be made here. The first concerns trends in social security spending. In the longer term, there has been a big rise, but this was from a small base in the early twentieth century (about 4.5 per cent of GNP in 1921). The rise was more noticeable in the decades after Second World War than it has been in the past 20 years or so (both sets of statistics, *The Guardian*, 21 October 1997). More recently, figures for 1978/79 to 1999/2000 (estimates) show a pattern fluctuating between 9 per cent and 13 per cent of national income spent on social security. It is currently falling from the peak achieved in the early 1990s, mainly because this peak was associated with the high unemployment of the recession.

The second observation here is a European comparison. In 1995, Britain was ninth out of 11 countries analysed for the amount of money spent per head on social protection benefits (*Social Trends*, 1998).

The dependency culture model

This is the idea that the more that the state does for people, the less they do for themselves. Not only that, but a lifestyle and set of values grows up that reinforces what became known as 'giro culture'. The root of the problem is said to be that benefits are too generous and are too easy to get, either legally or otherwise.

The model is premised on strongly individualist assumptions about society and the economy. These assumptions include the view that people can, and should, look after themselves rather than look to the state for support. Critics question both the 'can' and the 'should' parts of this argument.

From a sociological perspective, the 'can' part is dubious because it depends on the jobs and resources being available for people to be able to look after themselves. From a competing ideological perspective, social democrats would argue that the 'should' part is also wrong. They say that it is the mark of a civilised society that support for those in need is a collective responsibility.

Because the model is sometimes focussed on lone parents, it is worth looking at some recent research on this issue. In 1998, an Oxford University study of lone mothers and benefits between 1993 and 1997 was published. Using social security records of 7,000 claimants, it showed that 80 per cent of those on benefit in 1993 came off it at some point, or points, by 1997 – even if some reverted to benefit later. In short, up to four out of five had probably found work of their own accord. Significantly, those who had been 'teenage mums' were no more likely to stay on benefit than others. Only 2 per cent of the sample were teenagers, anyway. This does not suggest a large-scale tendency to welfare dependency (*The Guardian*, 23 April 1998). Other research, carried out by the Policy Studies Institute for the Department of Social Security, is also relevant here. This pointed to the problem of longstanding poor health, rather than dependency culture, as a factor in obtaining work. A longitudinal study, from 1991 to 1995, of 950 lone parents showed that the incidence of longstanding poor health in this group had risen from 15 per cent to 29 per cent (*The Guardian*, 16 April, 1998).

Activity
Find a list of up-to-date benefit levels. These might come from a Citizen's Advice Bureau, a post office or a Social Security Office. Consider the view that the benefit levels are high enough to generate a dependency culture.

Case studies on the themes of welfare abuse, burden and dependency

Case studies are extremely useful in sociology. Through studies of a particular group, event or institution, 'it may be that some broad generalisation is brought to life.' (McNeill, 1990). It is not usually thought that case studies can be used to test generalisations, but they can be in some circumstances, as the affluent-worker study showed (Goldthorpe and Lockwood, 1969).

These two observations give some idea of what the following case studies are for. First, they provide some empirical illustration of the general debates on welfare models. Second, they can be seen as tests of these general ideas. If they do not provide supporting evidence for the arguments in the three models discussed, these models have to be rejected as lacking general applicability.

Case Study 1: family needs and benefit levels
It is part of the dependency culture argument that benefit levels are too generous. There is, of course, a value-judgement element to this that cannot be challenged without another, alternative value judgement. However, empirical research can provide the basis on which value judgements are made. With this in mind, it is worth looking at the analysis of 30 existing studies, along with new research based on interviews with 2,100 people, all considering life on low incomes (Kempson, 1996a). The conclusion was that benefit levels were significantly below what families needed for 'basic essentials'. For a family of four, with two children aged between two and five, the gap was over £11 per week; in 1994, the food spend allocation for each child of these ages was £9.36 per week.

This confirms the findings of similar research in 1993, which showed that a family of four would have needed £23 above weekly Income Support rates to meet minimum needs for housing, food, fuel and clothing (CPAG, *The Cost of a Child*, 1993).

Case Study 2: sickness, disability and the burden model of welfare
One of the population groups with the fastest growth in claimant numbers has been that of the long-term sick and disabled. For example, the numbers of people receiving disability benefit doubled in 10 years to 1.5 million, increasing the cost from £1.5 billion to £5 billion (*The Guardian*, 14 June 1993). This led to two sets of accusations.

The first was when the Labour opposition accused the then Conservative Government's Employment Department of deliberately encouraging the process of unemployed people being signed off as sick or disabled so as to massage the unemployment figures downwards.

The second was when the then Conservative Social Security Department later accused family doctors of being too ready to sign people off work as sick or disabled. One reason why doctors were allegedly doing this was that it was in their patients' interests to be on these more generous benefits. It was the very cost of doing this, however, that worried the Social Security Department.

As a result of concerns like these, the government changed the benefit rules. Invalidity Benefit payable after 28 weeks of statutory National Insurance sick pay was replaced by Incapacity Benefit. There was a much more rigorous medical test to qualify for this; ie it became harder to get.

In the House of Commons, the Social Security Secretary, Peter Lilley, said:

Those who are working for a modest wage resent seeing neighbours, apparently as fit as themselves, living on invalidity benefit. It has become popularly known as 'bad back' benefit.

Study point
In what ways does this quotation illustrate any of the three different models of welfare that feature in the account of the 'welfare backlash'?

Footnote – proposed changes to Invalidity Benefit, 1999

A highly controversial issue emerged in May 1999 when the government proposed certain changes to disability benefits. One in particular was the idea to means-test National Insurance Invalidity Benefit. Critics said that this was an attack on disabled people and on the universalist principle of NI benefits, already eroded by the replacement of Unemployment Benefits with Jobseekers' Allowance (see p. 131). Government supporters argued that there are cost and needs issues to be considered. Claims for this type of benefit are rising while those from the unemployed, single parents and families with children are falling; 7 per cent of the working age population are on this benefit. Additionally, nearly half of Invalidity Benefit claimants are in the top 40 per cent of the income range (P. Toynbee, *The Guardian*, 14 May 1999).

THE CONSERVATIVE GOVERNMENT IN ACTION

The central aim of the Thatcher government was to 'roll back the state', to get individuals to do more for themselves and the government to do less. Key policies in this strategy included the following:

Privatisation and contracting out

A range of state industries were sold to the private owners, often at a very cheap price. It was not just that these industries were supposed to be more efficient in the private sector, where the profit motive was said to provide a spur to productivity. It was also that the money raised by their sale enabled taxes to be reduced. These tax cuts mainly favoured the better off (see p. 13). In addition, many public sector services were contracted out to private companies because it was believed that they could be run more efficiently. Significantly perhaps, the High Court decided in 1997 that the Conservative Government had deliberately broken the law by refusing to protect the wages and conditions of workers in contracted-out industries when they were put out to tender. In total, millions of pounds will be paid in compensation to the workers affected (*The Guardian*, 11 November 1997). In 1999, the Court of Appeal ruled that the newly privatised electricity companies 'had unlawfully plundered their pension funds' (*The Independent*, 11 February 1999) in order to finance redundancies and reduce their financial liabilities. As a result of the ruling, the whole power industry may have to 'pay back' as much as £1.5 billion into workers' pension funds, helping retired workers by as much as £10-15 per week. For more on the issue of privatisation, see Kempson, (1996b).

The promotion of private welfare

Incentives to opt into private welfare or health schemes were introduced. Tax subsidies were given to retired people if they were paying for private health insurance. The enormous encouragement given to people to opt out of their existing pension schemes and take out private ones created a huge scandal as many insurance companies gave misleading advice to prospective customers. Companies are now paying out millions in compensation. The rhetoric of promoting private welfare was not always matched by actual reforms or changes, however. In 1979, 48 per cent of spending on welfare services (social security, housing and education) had some private involvement; by 1986, this had only risen to 51 per cent (Joseph Rowntree Foundation, cited in *The Guardian*, 11 February 1999).

De-regulation

Minimum-wage protection in law was abolished for young people and for workers in low-wage industries covered by Wages Councils.

Trade union controls

Trade union powers were massively weakened by a series of laws, by mass unemployment and by the year-long conflict leading to the defeat of the miners in 1984/85. In neo-liberal ideology, trade unions are seen as limiting the free movement of market forces by artificially restricting the supply of labour.

Tax and welfare changes

There were many changes in benefit levels and entitlement, with a particular aim of 'targeting' benefits on the less well off. Some of the reforms were almost just changes of name from the existing system. Others, however, were real in their impact, with some groups being particularly hard hit, especially the young. Some of the main changes took place in 1988, and are listed below:

1 Supplementary Benefit (National Assistance until 1967) was renamed Income Support in 1988. Simultaneously, Income Support for 16/17 year olds was abolished, and the rate of benefit for under-25s was reduced.
2 The Social Fund was set up in 1988 to replace the additional and exceptional payments under the old system. Claimants were given discretionary grants or loans to meet their needs, or were referred to charities. The fund was cash limited, so claims might be refused, even if the case was genuine and strong.
3 Family Income Supplement was re-named Family Credit.

Other changes occurred over subsequent years. Often these were quite technical, such as in the rules governing claims for Housing Benefit, but their consequences were nonetheless substantial. Two examples of changes proposed in March 1997 can illustrate the sorts of change referred to. First, Housing Benefit was changed so that people under 60 living alone in rented accommodation would only qualify for a level of benefit equivalent to the rent of a room in a shared house. Two bedrooms is obviously excessive! Second, help with funeral costs from the Social Fund was changed so that it was denied to poor families unless they could prove that all immediate relatives were on social security.

Unemployment Benefit was also changed. Under the 1946 Act, entitlement to this expired after 12 months, but it was replaced by Jobseeker's Allowance in 1996. For six months only, this is available as a contributory benefit under the National Insurance system. After that, it becomes a means-tested benefit, effectively replacing Income Support for the unemployed.

Tax changes over the period tended to make the system more regressive. It did this by a shift from direct to indirect taxation and by making big reductions in the rates of income tax for top earners.

THE INFLUENCE OF EUROPE ON SOCIAL WELFARE

Not all pressures for welfare changes in this period were for reduced welfare provision. From the late 1970s onwards, changes in British social policy have sometimes come from the obligations of membership of the European Union rather than from domestic social or political considerations. One of the main influences has been the European requirement for equal treatment for women and men in social legislation.

- One early example of this was women acquiring the right to claim Supplementary Benefit and Family Income Supplement on behalf of themselves and their male partners. To do this, a women has to be, or to have been, the main breadwinner, but prior to this ruling, the only circumstance where a women could claim for a male partner as a dependant was if he were disabled.
- Another example was the requirement to equalise the ages at which women and men acquire the right to a state retirement pension. Pensions are discussed in Chapter 4 (see pp. 74–80).
- More recently, it has been announced that parents will be given legal rights to time off work to look after sick children, though it is thought that, in most cases, it will be women who will use this right (*The Guardian*, 4 May 1998).
- In late 1998, the Government announced that Widows' Benefit, a National Insurance benefit payable to widows over 45 without dependent children, was to be reformed. In effect, it was to be scrapped and replaced by a bereavement allowance, payable only for six months instead of until retirement, though it would not affect those already in receipt of Widows' Benefit. The new allowance would go to widowers as well as widows and would thereby equalise treatment of women and men, but it was likely to be targeted on

those on low incomes rather than to be universal. The change anticipated a European Court ruling on the issue that was expected to rule that the existing benefit was discriminatory.

- In 1999, a ruling at the European Court of Justice found that the 'habitual residence test' contravened the European Union principle of freedom of movement within the EU. The Conservatives had introduced the test in 1994 to act against so-called 'benefit tourists' who were allegedly coming to Britain to exploit its welfare system. In fact, it particularly hit people who had left Britain to temporarily work abroad or who had taken extended holidays overseas, often affecting black and Asian Britons the most. 100,000 people were disadvantaged by it, three-quarters of them British nationals. In May 1999, benefit offices were instructed to consider someone returning 'to resume previous residence' as 'habitually resident' and, therefore, entitled to social security, according to their circumstances.

4 THE 1997 LABOUR GOVERNMENT

The Labour government came into office saying that it would keep to the overall level of public spending and direct taxation that the previous Conservative Government had laid out for two years. However, this did not stop it planning

THE MAIN GROUP TO BE TARGETED BY THE LABOUR GOVERNMENT'S 'NEW DEAL' SCHEME WERE THE YOUNG (18–24 YRS) UNEMPLOYED.

and introducing a series of welfare reforms of some significance. It was too early, at the time of writing, to know all the details of these policies, still less their outcomes. However, some details had emerged in time to be included.

The slogan, 'Welfare to Work', was a central theme in many of these policies, linked to the accompanying policy title of the 'New Deal'. The aim was to reduce poverty and the cost of welfare by encouraging and enabling more social security recipients to find employment. Sometimes, this encouragement involved an element of compulsion, as in the requirement for new social security claimants to attend job advice interviews. The Social Security Secretary argued that such interviews were part of the process of challenging the 'poverty of ambition and poverty of expectation', as well as of asserting the responsibilities of claimants, rather than just their rights (*The Guardian*, 11 February 1999). This reference to welfare cultures shows that the welfare ideologies referred to above cannot be seen as fixed, or as automatically linked to particular political parties.

The main groups to be targeted by the Welfare to Work policy included lone parents, the unemployed and the long-term sick and disabled. The total cost was estimated to be about £4 billion over four years.

Before looking at these schemes in more detail, it is worth recalling the early introduction of a national minimum wage for those in work, even if at a lower level than trade unions wanted.

Lone parents

The aim of this policy is to reduce the proportion of lone parents dependent on benefits, a level which had risen from 44 per cent to almost 70 per cent under the Conservatives (*The Guardian*, 4 July 1997). The policy itself is based on research showing that many lone parents want to work rather than be on benefit. For example, a study of nearly 7,000 lone mothers by Oxford University's department of applied social studies found overwhelming evidence that these women wanted to work, especially the younger mothers (*The Guardian*, 23 April 1998). This does not fit the stereotypes sometimes projected by media reports.

The policy introduces the idea of interviews, advice, training and help with child-care costs to help get lone mothers into employment.

Critics have come in various forms. Feminists have expressed concern at the possibility of compulsion being included in the scheme, making mothers leave their children when they do not wish to, or making them take unsuitable jobs. The government has denied that there will be any such compulsion to work, though interviews with job advisors may be obligatory. PSI research, referred to earlier, indicated high levels of illness among lone parents, suggesting that returning to work will be difficult for some (*The Guardian*, 16 April 1998).

Unemployment

The New Deal for the unemployed started in April 1998, and concentrated most on the young, though long-term unemployed adults were also later incorporated into it. The main plank of this policy is to transfer part of the benefits of the unemployed to employers as an inducement to take them on as workers. Employers' labour costs are kept down, and the newly employed workers may later be able to obtain work at wages above their former benefit level. Other elements include a boost to training and education opportunities and working on environmental schemes or in the voluntary sector.

Points of evaluation – some assessment of Welfare to Work

Criticisms of the scheme have been varied, sometimes ideological and sometimes more pragmatic, focussing on the practicality of the scheme rather than its overall features.

It has been pointed out, for example, that the numbers of long-term unemployed peaked in 1993 and then fell rapidly as economic growth took the economy out of recession (**P. Robinson** of the Institute of Public Policy Research, *The Guardian*, 8 June 1998). This reinforces the Keynesian view of economist, R. Morris. He said that the way to reduce long-term unemployment and underclass dependency is:

---

not to be found in micro or social policies, such as Welfare to Work, but in the improved macro performance of economies.

The Guardian, 31 August 1998

In other words, he argues that economic policies should be about promoting social welfare by stimulating the demand for labour through economic growth. High levels of unemployment generally occur because of a shortage of jobs, not because the unemployed are unemployable.

One of the problems with the Welfare to Work scheme is that there are regional variations in unemployment and in employment opportunities. A private research agency called Income Data Services noted that, in the areas of high unemployment, the required job placements would be in the shortest supply. In these areas, such as the North and Scotland:

---

participants will end up in the voluntary sector or on an environmental task force rather than in paid employment.

The Guardian, 4 March 1998

Initial data on the impact of the New Deal on the young unemployed has been difficult to interpret. A year after it started, the unemployment rate was at its lowest since 1980, and employment was growing faster than unemployment was falling, indicating that people were coming out of economic inactivity into work.

Youth unemployment fell by 35 per cent between January 1998 and February 1999, and it was notable that this fall was fastest among those who qualified for Welfare to Work schemes. However, this fall started before the schemes started. In short, the New Deal may have had a positive impact on youth unemployment but so too had a buoyant labour market, especially in lower-paid, service sector jobs (*The Guardian*, 4 March 1999).

The Working Families Tax Credit (WFTC) and other support for families with children

In the March 1998 Budget, the introduction of this 'new' benefit was announced. In fact, its newness is only partial because it is really an expansion of the existing Family Credit system to include 400,000 additional families. Its aim, in line with the new benefits ethos, is to make working more financially attractive by increasing the supplement to earned incomes that this benefit gives. It should be in operation by late 1999 and, following the 1999 Budget, at a more generous level than originally announced and much more generous than Family Credit.

Other support for families with children came with higher-than-inflation increases in Child Benefit rates and a new tax allowance. This comes from the abolition of the Married Couple's Allowance (in 1999) and its replacement a year later with a new tax credit for families with children, worth nearly double the allowance it replaces. One concern expressed about WFTC and, more especially, the new child tax allowance is that it is likely to go through the wage packet rather than directly to the caring parent, most likely the mother.

Disability

As seen above, there are considerable problems in defining what counts as incapacity for work and in trying to deal with the possibility that many recipients of incapacity benefit are really able to work. The disability lobby (the pressure groups campaigning on behalf of the disabled) was very active in persuading the government that most people on the various disability benefits were justifiably receiving their benefits. In terms of 'Welfare to Work' for those with disabilities, therefore, the government adopted a rather gradualist approach. A new feature to the benefit system will be a requirement that all *new* claimants attend an interview with personal advisers on jobs and training; this is similar to the scheme for lone parents. The scheme is due to start on a pilot basis and to apply nationally from April 2000.

A disabled person's tax credit, replacing the disability working allowance, was announced in the Queenn's Speech of Labour's policy intentions for 1999. It has similar aims to the Working Families Tax Credit referred to above.

See also p. 129, the footnote dealing with the Labour Government's 1999 to means-test Invalidity Benefit.

Study point
What criticism would a traditional Marxist be likely to make of the Welfare to Work schemes above?

Pensions

This section needs to be read in conjunction with the earlier section on retirement pensioners in Chapter 4 (see pp. 74–80).

The main pension policy announcement from Labour came in 1999 when it declared that SERPS would be scrapped. In its place will be a second state pension to top up the basic National Insurance pension. This second pension is seen as mainly for those on incomes below £9,000, who will be guaranteed a minimum income of 20 per cent of average earnings, and *this will rise in step with average earnings* (the Budget, 1999). Above that income but below £18,500, the second state pension will remain available, but people will be encouraged to take out private 'stakeholder' pensions to top up the basic state pension. The value of the latter will continue to rise only in line with prices, not wages. People on incomes above this are not much affected by the changes. Indeed, tax relief on private pension contributions remains the same. This means that a higher-rate taxpayer pays only 60p for each £1 that goes into their pension scheme – the remaining 40p comes from the tax that they would otherwise have paid.

One other set of changes announced was the decision to give pension credits to people who had not had the chance to acquire them through work. This includes those looking after relatives and children under 5, as well as long-term disabled people with broken employment records. This will help up to 4 million people by 2050, most of them women.

Points of evaluation

The old age lobby was generally critical of the lack of radicalism in the scheme, but carers' organisations welcomed it.

Some critics argued that there was no incentive for the 'Jack the Lad' to take out additional pensions if their retirement income was already guaranteed (Frank Field in *The Independent*, 16 December 1998). Others noted that the scheme guaranteed that a minimum income will be means-tested and, therefore, will still have the stigma that Income Support does today.

The general level of benefits

Of course, there are people for whom work is not an option at all, and a different welfare strategy from welfare to work has to be adopted for them. The discussion here looks at this situation in terms of a general issue, benefit levels, and afterwards at a more specific one, pensions.

Not long after coming into office, Labour announced that it would not reverse the decision taken by the Thatcher government to cut the link between benefits and earnings and up-rate benefits annually only in line with prices. This means that people on benefits will have no increase in their real standard of living, regardless of how fast people in work improve theirs (Glyn, 1997). This last point was strongly emphasised in a Joseph Rowntree report written by the head of the LSE's unit for the analysis of social exclusion. (Hills, 1998). Unless benefits are increased in line with earnings rather than prices, Piachaud estimates that there could be an increase in poverty under Labour of 1.5 million by the next election (Piachaud, 1988).

As has been seen, some benefits have been increased faster than inflation, and the situation of retirement pensions needs to be remembered when this is considered.

CONCLUSION

Clearly, there are many changes to social policy that are yet to be decided and the outcomes of already announced ones are yet to be seen. The questions that sociologists and students of welfare will be interested in when analysing these policies will include the following:

1 What impact do they have on the numbers in, or on the margins of, poverty?
2 Does their financing reduce the degree of income inequality in society, increase it or leave it unchanged?
3 More particularly, how do they affect the level of inequality based on age, gender, ethnicity and disability?
4 Are their underlying ideologies detectable in the way benefits are organised, such as those based on traditional gender assumptions, on ideas of the deserving/undeserving poor, and on images of welfare as burden or of claimants as potential malingerers?
5 What degree of social control, or even coercion, is built into the welfare system?

SUMMARY

- State welfare provision is partly about dealing with the inadequacies of the market in providing solutions to social problems and individual needs. However, this welfare provision has often been influenced by a desire not to interfere too heavily with market forces, even at the expense of the level and quality of that provision.
- This tension between state provision and leaving things to market forces is one of the major historical and ideological themes in the sociology of welfare provision.
- Part of this tension is about whether state welfare provision should generally be provided on a universal basis, like the state National Insurance pension, or selectively on the basis of a means-test, such as with Housing Benefit.

- This ideological tension is fed into by economic concerns about the cost of welfare, expressed in debates about the ageing population or the growth in the number of single parents on benefit.
- There are other ideological conflicts over the nature of welfare, such as the extent to which benefits reinforce traditional gender role assumptions or are based on economic policies destructive of the environment.
- Generally, the immediate postwar period was the high point in the development of collectively provided universal welfare benefits, and the Conservative years of the 1980s/90s the period when they were most under direct attack.
- The Labour Government of 1997 has placed enormous stress on solving welfare needs by getting more people into employment, though there have been policies for those for whom this is not appropriate, such as the retired.
- The effectiveness of welfare must be measured against such indicators of success or failure as the level of poverty, the extent of social exclusion and so on.

STUDY GUIDES

Practice questions

1 How successful has the welfare state been in eradicating poverty in modern Britain? Your answer to this question will require reference to Chapter 5 on poverty.
2 'Welfare provision is shaped as much by ideology as by people's needs.' Discuss.
3 To what extent is it justified to see the welfare state as a burden that cannot be afforded? Your answer to this question will benefit from reference to sections of Chapter 4 on elderly people in society.

Group work

Collect articles about welfare issues from the press and/or broadcast media over a specified period of time. Work in pairs or small groups, perhaps on particular media outlets (eg the popular press/broadsheets/papers that are traditionally Labour/Conservative/etc). Analyse the items around themes like the levels of benefit, costs of welfare, typical or stereotypical claimants, and the ideologies and models of welfare referred to above. Report findings to the rest of the group and note variations in pattern according to the outlet types dealt with.

Coursework suggestions

Design or carry out a piece of survey research that explores people's attitudes to various aspects of the welfare state. Either choose issues of significance from those covered here or topical ones from the news.

FURTHER READING

The following titles have been selected as useful for further reading or reference.

Adonis, A. and Pollard, S. (1988) *A Class Act – The Myth of Britain's Classless Society*, Penguin. This covers a wide range of issues about inequality in contemporary Britain, from health to politics, and does so in an extremely accessible way.

Alcock, P. (1996) *Social Policy in Britain – Themes and Issues*, Macmillan. This is for the student, or perhaps teacher, who wants to look at detailed social policy matters for charities to the European Union. It has some more difficult sections on background economic theories.

Amin, K. and Oppenheim, C. (1992) *Poverty in Black and White*, Child Poverty Action Group, London. This explores immigration, family patterns, labour-market inequalities, discrimination in social security and health issues in relation to poverty among Britain's ethnic minorities.

Arber, S. (1989) 'Class and the elderly', in *Social Studies Review*, January 1989, Philip Allan, Deddington, Oxfordshire. A little dated now but a very useful introduction to the issues in its title.

Barrat, D. and Cole, T. (1991) *Sociology Projects – A Students' Guide*, Routledge. Very useful for students wishing to find out more about how to carry out the suggested research and coursework activities.

British Social Attitudes, BSA/Dartmouth. An annual publication based on large-scale, random social surveys. It often deals with welfare issues, from attitudes to the state to the quality of housing. Essential for a good sociology library.

Cole, T. (1986) *Whose Welfare?* Tavistock. This provides some of the historical background on the history of the welfare state not included in this text.

Dennehy, A. et al (1997) *Not to be Ignored – Young People, Poverty and Health*, CPAG. A series of articles, some quite technical, on how poverty affects young people and how social policies can address this, including at the level of health and education.

General Household Survey, HMSO. Large-scale, official survey. Essential reference on a wide range of issues.

Ginn, J. and Arber, S. (1992) Philip Allan, Oxfordshire. 'Gender and resources in later life', *Sociology Review*, November 1992. A very useful and accessible amount of why gender is important in understanding old age and why welfare is not just about money.

Graham, H. (ed) (1985) *Health and Welfare*, Macmillan, London. A bit on the dated side now, but the value of this little book is found in the readings and extracts from a wide range of authors covering issues from the social construction of dependency in old age (Townsend) to Marxist theories of state welfare (Ginsberg).

Jordan, B. and Marsland, D. (1989) 'Face to Face', *Social Studies Review*, November 1989, Philip Allan. A little dated but still a useful contrast between two views on welfare means testing, written for an A level sociology journal.

McNeill, P. (1990) *Reserach Methods*, 2nd edn., Routledge. Very useful for students wishing to find out more about the research methods necessary for carrying out the suggested coursework activities.

Moore, S. (1998) *Social Welfare Alive!* 2nd edn., Stanley Thornes, Cheltenham. This is a very useful reference for the student who wants to obtain more detail on the administrative structure and specific patterns of welfare provision. It deals with issues as wide as the National Health Service and youth crime.

Oppenheim, C. and Harker, L. (1996) *Poverty – the Facts*, 3rd edn., CPAG. For the student or teacher who wants real detail on the extent and distribution of poverty.

Social Trends. Indisputable data on income, wealth, housing, demography and so on.

Spybey, T. (ed) (1997) *Britain in Europe – An Introduction to Sociology*, Routledge, London. Not an easy book for the new A level student, though sections are accessible enough. This covers a wide range of areas of sociological relevance to sociology and social policy in the context of contemporary Europe, including its social structure and its social policies on the family, the labour market and old people.

Walker, A. and Walker, C. (eds) *Britain Divided – The Growth of Social Exclusion in the 1980s and 1990s*, CPAG. This gives detailed empirical coverage of many issues of relevance here, from gender inequality to privatisation of public utilities.

Warde, A. and Abercrombie, N. (eds) (1994) *Stratification and Social Inequality*, Framework Press. This book contains chapters by different authors discussing the research methods and findings of a number of studies, including that by Saunders on housing, several on gender inequality in employment and one on inequality in Northern Ireland.

INDEX